Mastering Risk and Procurement in Project Management

A Guide to Planning, Controlling, and Resolving Unexpected Problems

Randal Wilson

Associate Publisher: Amy Neidlinger
Executive Editor: Jeanne Glasser Levine
Development Editor: Natasha Torres
Operations Specialist: Jodi Kemper
Cover Designer: Chuti Prasertsith
Managing Editor: Kristy Hart
Project Editors: Laura Hernandez, Elaine Wiley
Copy Editor: Language Logistics, LLC
Proofreader: Katie Matejka
Indexer: Erika Millen
Compositor: Nonie Ratcliff
Manufacturing Buyer: Dan Uhrig

Upper Saddle River, New Jersey 07458

For information about buying this title in bulk quantities, or for special sales opportunities (which may include electronic versions; custom cover designs; and content particular to your business, training goals, marketing focus, or branding interests), please contact our corporate sales department at corpsales@pearsoned.com or (800) 382-3419.

For government sales inquiries, please contact governmentsales@pearsoned.com.

For questions about sales outside the U.S., please contact international@pearsoned.com.

Company and product names mentioned herein are the trademarks or registered trademarks of their respective owners.

Printed in the United States of America

First Printing September 2014

ISBN-10: 0-13-383790-4
ISBN-13: 9-78-013383790-2

Pearson Education LTD.
Pearson Education Australia PTY, Limited.
Pearson Education Singapore, Pte. Ltd.
Pearson Education Asia, Ltd.
Pearson Education Canada, Ltd.
Pearson Educación de Mexico, S.A. de C.V.
Pearson Education—Japan
Pearson Education Malaysia, Pte. Ltd.

Library of Congress Control Number: 2014943267

*I would like to dedicate this book to my wife Dusty
and sons Nolan, Garrett, and Carlin
for their support and patience
through this project.*

Contents

Part II: Project Execution

Part III: Integrated Monitoring and Control

Part IV: Project Closer

About the Author

Randal Wilson, MBA, PMP, serves as Visiting Professor of Project Management, Keller Graduate School of Management, at the Elk Grove, CA DeVry University campus. His teaching style is one of addressing Project Management concepts using not only academic course guidelines and text, but includes in-depth discussions in lectures using practical application from industry experience.

Mr. Wilson is currently Operations and Project Manager at Parker Hose and Fittings. He is responsible for five locations across Northern California and Nevada, as well as project management of redesigns/renovation of existing facilities and construction of new facilities.

Mr. Wilson was formally in the telecommunications industry as Senior New Product Introduction Engineer at REMEC, Inc., Senior New Product Introduction Engineer with Spectrian Corp., and Associate Design Engineer with American Microwave Technology. He also served as Senior Manufacturing Engineer at Hewlett Packard.

He is a certified Project Management Professional (PMP) of the Project Management Institute. He acquired an MBA with a concentration in General Operations Management from Keller Graduate School of Management of DeVry University in Fremont, California, and a Bachelor of Science in Technical Management with a concentration in Project Management from DeVry University in Fremont.

Introduction

Manufacturing, distribution, sales, and service organizations have one thing in common: the requirement of *resources*. An organization's success, in many cases, is a direct function of how it obtains and manages resources to carry out its strategic business objectives. The organization's first and most important task is to obtain management personnel who are skilled and experienced in acquiring and managing resources, which may include:

- **Human resources**
- **Materials and supplies**
- **Equipment and facilities**
- **Transportation**
- **Finances**
- **Intellectual property**

In the process of obtaining resources within all organizations, either for daily operations or for special projects, there are two givens: Resources must be obtained, and they have the potential to be problematic. The challenge, then, is how to obtain the correct resources at the right time and for a cost equitable for the organization, as well as how to manage any potential problems that may occur with a given resource. *Mastering Risk and Procurement in Project Management* has been designed not only to explain basic concepts in risk and procurement management, but also to offer tools and techniques that can be used by a project manager, project staff, and supporting departments that would be associated with risk or procurement.

Problems Are Inevitable

As organizations utilize resources in daily operations and within projects, it becomes quickly evident that a variety of problems and issues can be associated with resources. Human resources are often the primary resources used across organizations. Given the potential of variability in skills, individualism, reliability, and work ethic, they can bring to the table an array of challenges and problems. An interesting component of human resources is that although people are often the source of a variety of problems, they also have the ability to solve them, which is typically not the case for other types of resources.

Problems can also be associated with other resources, such as materials and supplies. They can be incorrect, get damaged, or fail as a result of poor quality. Equipment and facilities can develop problems that can render them less effective or inoperable altogether. Some organizations can have financial challenges that make it difficult to fund projects, constraining project managers in their need to obtain and schedule resources for work activities.

Regardless of what type of resource is used, problems are inevitable, and the project manager must develop a system to deal with problems throughout the project lifecycle. As problems are not designed to happen on projects, they are typically characterized as having a potential to occur, which we commonly refer to as *risk*.

The second component of projects that inevitably develops problems is associated with purchasing items required for project work activities and acquiring subcontractors. The purchasing aspect of a project can itself introduce several types of problems and is in many cases connected to risk management. The area of purchasing and acquiring items for the project is commonly referred to as *conducting procurement*.

What Is Risk?

Risk is generally defined within project management as a potential influence producing a positive or negative outcome. We look at the definition of risk within the context of a project as any influence to a work activity that generates an outcome that was not expected.

EXAMPLE   A work activity is being performed outdoors, and poor weather is imminent.

Rain, in and of itself, is not necessarily bad; Earth requires rain, and on some days it can actually be relaxing. Rain becomes a problem if it impacts a work activity, such as damaging materials and supplies, rendering equipment inoperable, or simply forcing a shutdown, causing a schedule delay. The rain therefore has the potential to create an influence that can alter the outcome of a work activity, thus creating a problem. The rain is not designed as a normally scheduled part of work activity, so we consider it to be a potential "risk."

Bad Risk Versus Good Risk

Events or circumstances that have a potential to influence work activity can result in either a negative or a positive outcome. As we saw in the example, relative to a specific work activity, rain can present a bad risk. Another form of potential risk is the use of external human resources that have been subcontracted to perform work activity. These individuals not being a part of the organization can present issues such as difficulty in team environments, ignorance of organizational processes and culture, or personality conflict with management and staff they work with directly—all typically risks associated with a negative outcome. However, over time the same external resource might exhibit a much higher level of ability and knowledge, therefore completing the assigned task much more quickly and allowing the work activity to be ahead of schedule. So, although there is a potential risk in using subcontractors, their influence can also create a positive outcome.

Project managers should always have a conceptual understanding of risk—that although risks can generate negative outcomes, there are occasions where positive things come out of what was thought to be a potential negative risk. The project manager would then seek to exploit these positive outcomes to yield the maximum benefit for the project.

Risk Versus Uncertainty

As the project manager plans work activities and evaluates all the resources that are required, he begins to see where potential problems might insert themselves. This is where the project manager can begin to identify risks and possibly plan responses. As we have seen, some influences can be identified as "potential" problems and therefore can be planned for and worked around, but there are also issues and influences that cannot be anticipated and were nowhere on the radar. These are called *uncertainties*. Risks are influences that can be identified as having a potential to create a problem, whereas uncertainties are problems that happen that could not have been identified prior to the work activity.

EXAMPLE

An uncertainty might be in the case of an earthquake that could potentially damage a construction project. Although rain, tornadoes, lightning, mudslides, and earthquakes are often called acts of God and are the very definition of uncertainty, they can also be considered risks because our current technology can predict the potential of inclement weather, and thus they can be planned for to some degree. Uncertainty would be an influence that cannot be foreseen and that occurs without notice. In the case of a construction project, an uncertainty could be a massive earthquake that happens without notice, resulting in a negative outcome.

What Is Procurement?

Most projects require resources that are obtained through purchasing or subcontracting; this is called *conducting procurement*. Most organizations have individuals or entire departments dedicated to the task of purchasing what the organization needs to run its daily operations. When a project manager has outlined all of the work activities and resources required to complete each activity, she submits a list of all items that need to be purchased and/or contracted through-out the project lifecycle. Procurements can be classified into two general categories: items that need to be purchased and resources that must be managed through a contract agreement.

- **Purchases**

  Items that need to be obtained for project activities are simply purchased through suppliers or vendors. This can be accomplished by the purchasing agent selecting items through a catalog or website, contacting the supplier/vendor, placing the order, establishing delivery requirements, and agreeing on payment terms and conditions. As soon as the item has been delivered and it is confirmed that it meets expectations, payment can be made and the transaction closed.

- **Contracts**

  Another form of obtaining resources is the use of a contract agreement. In many cases, contracts are used to acquire external human resources needed for special tasks on work activities or perhaps the lease of equipment or facilities that will be used on work activities. As there is a certain amount of risk for both the buyer and seller in acquiring these type of resources, outlining the conditions of the contract is important and must cover the following:

  - Scope of work to be performed
  - Specific identification of a piece of equipment or facility
  - Terms of its use or environment
  - Duration that the buyer plans to have the resource
  - Agreed upon price
  - Special terms or conditions that would address risk for the buyer or seller

  An agreement signed by both parties forms a legal binding contract requiring both parties to fulfill their responsibilities identified in the document(s).

Risks and Procurement Go Hand-in-Hand

Risks associated with various aspects of the project might include correctly interpreting the customer's requirements for a deliverable, selecting projects that are appropriate for the organization, and availability of resources within the organization to carry out project work activities, but there are also risks associated in the process of conducting procurement. Most projects require items to be purchased and/or some form of contract agreement that will have the potential of introducing risk. This being the case, why are risks associated with things that have to be purchased?

- **Risk Is a Threshold Within Procurement**—The fundamental philosophy regarding risk is the identification of a potential problem that might or might not happen. When the purchasing agent is tasked with obtaining an item from a supplier/vendor, there are three primary components that determine the transaction's success:
  - *Buyer's Responsibility*—To start the transaction, the purchasing agent must ensure he has all the information required to correctly identify what needs to be purchased. He must also identify a seller that can provide the item in the correct form, fit, and function; at a reasonable price; and within time constraints. If the purchasing agent has correctly identified a seller that can fulfill these requirements, the transaction can be initiated. The purchasing agent, project manager, or other staff must confirm delivery of the item and that it has met all identified requirements. The purchasing agent must then ensure that full payment has been made, and the transaction can be closed.
  - *Seller's Responsibility*—In response to an inquiry by a purchasing agent, the seller is responsible for ensuring she understands all of the requirements of the item that is intended to be purchased. The seller must inform the buyer of any special options associated with a particular item that the company offers as well as verify her ability to get it to the buyer. The seller must be truthful that the offered item meets *all* requirements communicated by the buyer and not

mislead for purposes of making the sale. The seller must also verify pricing is correct and be upfront about any extra fees or costs applied—such as shipping and handling, and/or tax—to give the buyer the full actual cost of the item. The seller must also be diligent in ensuring the item is delivered to the intended location by the date she committed to and packaged in such a way that the item will not be damaged during shipment.

- *Delivery Responsibility*—As the purchased item leaves the seller's location and is in transit to the buyer's location, the responsibility lies with the organization contracted to deliver it. As the seller has a responsibility to correctly package an item for delivery, it is the delivery company's responsibility to ensure the item is not damaged in transit, regardless if the item's destination is a third party, the buyer, or the seller.

As we have seen in these primary components of successfully managing the transaction of procuring an item and having it successfully delivered and being correct in form, fit, and function, we can see that risk is associated with every aspect of conducting procurement. We can look at procurement as having a level, or threshold, of risk associated with it, and this is why risk and procurement go hand-in-hand.

In the case where the purchasing agent is using a contract agreement to obtain an external resource, there will also be a buyer/seller relationship, and in some cases a delivery component required. The same buyer/seller responsibilities exist within a contract and can even include the complication of special terms and conditions the can add even more risk in using contracted resources.

We know procurement is part of every project to some degree, and given the nature of things that have to be purchased or contracted, procurement can introduce a large component of risk throughout the project lifecycle. The project manager must be aware that the procurement process can generate potential problems and that he must work closely with those involved in procurement to manage risks associated with it.

Seeing Is Believing

As the project manager begins to develop the project plan, which includes breaking down the project deliverables into their smallest components, understanding all resources that are required, estimating costs, and scheduling, she begins to see where potential problems may occur that could have impact on the project. The most important tool a project manager could have in managing projects is seeing problems ahead of time and being prepared with responses. When the project manager can see areas of potential problems and can plan for these problems, she becomes a believer that risk can be managed if planned for correctly.

Risk and Procurement—Planned?

Most project managers will agree that certain responses that were planned ahead of time saved or protected not only a project activity, but also the schedule or perhaps even the project's budget. Planning for risks allows for the project manager and staff to have a response ready in case a problem occurs. This can mean the difference between having the time to design the best response possible versus having no time and making knee-jerk reactions that will simply put a Band-Aid on the problem and generally be a more expensive solution. Project managers, in planning for risk with well-designed responses, can actually be one of the project's biggest assets in protecting not only the project but also the organization from problems that could be anywhere from minor to having a catastrophic impact.

Save the Project and Organization

A project manager has a responsibility to ensure the completion of all work activities that produce the project deliverable, which in turn meets the expectations of the project objective. He also has the authority to plan and manage all of the work activities, as well as the responsibility to plan for and manage risk throughout the project lifecycle. If the project manager is seen as the individual who ensures the outcome of the project deliverable, he can also be seen as the individual who might ultimately save the project from its own problems through *risk management*.

In some cases the project manager has not only saved the project budget, schedule, and quality of the deliverable, but has protected the organization from legal action that might have been a possibility through certain contract agreements but was managed in a risk response. Project managers and purchasing agents within the procurement department know that the use of contracts and how they are negotiated can be used as a risk management tool—and can accordingly mitigate or eliminate risks associated with a bigger picture regarding the entire organization in regard to potential legal actions.

Proactive Versus Reactive

As we've stated, one of the most powerful tools the project manager can have is visibility of all potential risks and a best-case-scenario risk response planned for each of them ahead of time. Unfortunately, as projects are developed, project managers can find themselves very busy, and identifying and planning risk responses will either be a lesser priority or will not be completed at all. This is unfortunate, as we can see in Figure I.1. Failing to plan for risks can ultimately have an impact on the project deliverable, budget, and schedule.

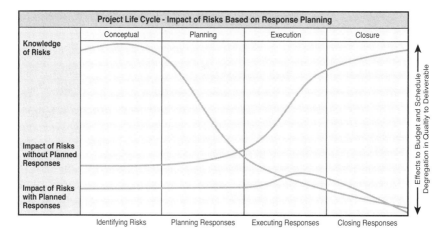

Figure I.1   Impact to Project with and without Risk Planning

When project managers are trying to manage work activities, issues arise on a regular basis that he must deal with. Some are minor, simply just making the decision of one thing over another, while in other cases a problem has actually occurred and needs a response and corrective action. When the project manager has no time to think of a best-case scenario response, "reacting" to a problem indicates the problem has already occurred and the project manager is simply performing damage control.

Project managers discipline themselves to allocate time before a project starts to identify potential problems, predict the probability of occurrence, analyze potential impact to the project, and use resources available to identify best case scenario responses. This is an example of working in a "proactive" response mode. When project managers are proactive in response planning, they have a roadmap of potential problems and are almost *waiting* for them to occur. From this position, in some cases the project manager and project staff can actually make alterations to a work activity prior to a potential risk to simply eliminate it. Being proactive in risk identification and response planning gives the project manager confidence throughout the project lifecycle that they can not only see problems before they happen, but they have an opportunity to eliminate them, or, at worst, have a response for a best-case scenario outcome that is in the best interest of the project in the organization.

Problem Management Versus Change Management

Although project managers do the best they can in identifying potential "problems" that may occur throughout the project lifecycle, the one uncertainty project managers cannot plan for are any changes that will be required throughout the project lifecycle. As we have seen, when the project manager operates in a proactive mode, it is because she has developed a process that outlines steps to take in certain scenarios. As we have seen, developing a risk management plan is a process the project manager can follow to consistently deal with potential problems. Another process the project manager can use is to address changes required throughout the project lifecycle.

Some project managers view change as a problem—and therefore a risk—that should be mitigated or eliminated. A customer might make a request to alter something on the project deliverable before it is completed so it will meet newly discovered conditions. As much as we would love to have the customer understand "all" specifications required for their deliverable at the beginning of a project, in some situations the customer may be working within a developing environment, and alterations to the deliverable might have to be made in order for it to work correctly in what the customer is developing. In this case, allowing for a project deliverable to be changed on the fly would be seen as good customer service.

In other cases, items that are procured might have to be altered slightly depending on availability or work required by an externally subcontracted resource. These types of changes are also inevitable but should be seen as opportunities to perfect what the project is trying to accomplish, rather than as an obstacle. Like any other aspect of the project, the project manager should develop a *change management process* to ensure changes are conducted correctly and efficiently and are implemented with minimal impact to the project. A detailed change management process is introduced later in this book. Project managers can use this powerful tool to control how change is managed on projects.

Is the Project Manager a Risk?

As we have seen throughout this introduction, there are several aspects regarding the management of project risk and procurement that the project manager either has direct responsibility for or will be involved in to some degree. Because the project manager has several responsibilities, such as the development of the project work breakdown structure, estimating a budget, and developing a project schedule, we can see that the project manager can pose a risk to the project based on his own knowledge, experience, and skill set—yes, a project manager himself can be a risk!

In some cases, the organization does not employ professional project managers to oversee projects but simply chooses a functional manager or someone else within the organization to oversee project activities. In this condition, the manager selected to oversee a project can cause several problems as a result of mismanagement. Even professional project managers hired within the organization to officially develop and manage projects have a wide variety of experience and skill sets, and they can introduce potential problems throughout the project lifecycle.

As more organizations see how the benefits of properly managed projects far outweighs the damage control resulting from projects with budget overruns, delayed schedules, and incorrectly developed project deliverables, they realize how important it is to select a project manager with the skills and experience to properly develop and manage a project. And when an organization understands that successes and failures on a project are not only the result of the project manager's abilities and work ethic, but is a result of everyone's efforts, including the project staff and supporting departments, a culture of effective risk management can be felt throughout the organization. This culture of risk awareness, with everyone considering risk management a part of his or her job, can be one of the strongest assets the project can have.

Organizational Culture of Risk Planning

Organizations in which projects are a large component of the business strategy have an understanding of the potential impact risks can have on not only projects, but throughout the organization—and so they often have a strong risk awareness culture. Organizations that are structured with functional departments that carry out day-to-day operations that do not necessarily function on a project basis and are not intimately associated with the organization's business on the whole, can struggle with the concept of risk management in how problems on a project can affect an organization.

Regardless of the organization structure, a project manager assigned to oversee a project must ensure certain project processes are developed and will be used throughout the project lifecycle. This is important, as processes are used to outline what is required as well as to ensure consistency in the process. As the project manager is addressing the area of risk and procurement on a project, she must also ensure processes are in place to manage these items.

- **Risk and Procurement as a Process**—As an organization matures with the use of projects, hopefully staff within the organization is also seeing the benefit of processes used to manage risk and procurement throughout a project lifecycle. The benefit of developing a process is it provides a step-by-step instruction to conduct items, which is important to effectively manage what the process is developed for. This book includes processes that can be used in managing all aspects of risk, as well as procurement on most types of projects. Although these can be simple processes, they can be used on complex projects and in their simplicity can be easily understood by not only a project manager but by other project staff that may be assisting with project tasks. It is important that the development of a process remain simple, as the fundamental steps can be used on either simple projects or complex projects, but those using the process will not lose sight of the overall concept of what the process is trying to accomplish.

- **PMBOK Processes**—The Project Management Institute (PMI) has published a book called *A Guide to the Project Management Body of Knowledge* (PMBOK Guide) that is used worldwide as a standard project managers can follow that will assist in the understanding of processes used throughout all aspects of managing projects. Several processes regarding risk and procurement management called out in the PMBOK are used in this text for general conceptual understanding of risk and procurement management and, in many cases, are explained in further detail and with the use of examples in regard to specific applications.

- **Documentation**—As the project manager develops the overall project management plan, there are several individual plans included that outline all of the process steps required for each aspect of the overall project. Other documents used in the organization that will house information regarding project activities may include documents within the Accounting department, Procurement department, Project Management Office (PMO), and Human Resources, as well as general documents such as a Lessons Learned document included with the completion of each project. With regard to risk management and procurement management, there are two primary documents used in the project management plan that outline all specific steps required for each of these two areas, which include:

- *Risk Management Plan*—Houses all of the information regarding how risk is to be managed throughout the project lifecycle. This includes identification of risk, analysis of risk, response plans, documentation of risk and responses, and any staff identified to assist in managing risk throughout the project lifecycle. The risk management plan also includes all of the processes used and specific steps required to correctly and effectively carry out each aspect of managing risk. The project manager is typically the owner and manager of the risk management plan for each project and would be the individual responsible for developing the plan and/or any modifications or additions to the plan throughout the project lifecycle.

- *Procurement Management Plan*—Houses all of the information regarding how procurement should be conducted throughout the project lifecycle. This plan is typically developed as a joint effort between the project manager, the Procurement department, and sometimes the Accounting department. It houses all of the processes required to correctly and effectively carry out procurement throughout the project lifecycle. This can include conducting purchases, negotiating contracts, any specific pricing schedules that might be required, as well as roles and responsibilities required to negotiate contracts and effectively conduct procurement. This document can be developed by either the project manager or the procurement manager, and both of these individuals will need to have a clear understanding of the development of processes within the procurement management plan; roles and responsibilities of management overseeing aspects of procurement; and the management of human resources that will be conducting procurement and accounting functions. The important aspect here is that all processes required are included in the procurement management plan, and that everyone involved in this plan is on the same page as to the understanding of the processes included.

- *Lessons Learned*—Another important document that is used throughout project management is the Lessons Learned document used to record not only problems relative to risk management and/or procurement, but successes due to processes that were designed and implemented, resulting in a positive outcome. The Lessons Learned document is typically regarded as an important document within project management, as project managers use this document at the beginning stages of developing a project to avoid problems that have occurred on prior projects.

  Project managers can use valuable information from prior projects in the development of the risk management plan in identifying potential problems and successful responses of problems that occurred on prior projects. This can save the project manager a great deal of time (and in some cases, guesswork) as to what a successful response to a particular risk might be. Project managers can also use the Lessons Learned document to gain valuable information on prior purchases or the use of subcontractors to avoid problems or issues seen on past projects. This can, in some cases, save the organization a great deal of money and time in selecting a more appropriate response to a risk over a response that might have made more sense if other details of the risk had been unknown. Lessons Learned documents have proven to be a valuable source of information for the project manager in developing the project management plan and should always be a document every project manager develops and uses throughout the project lifecycle to record information that would be valuable for later use.

In many ways, the success of a project manager can be boiled down to the simple fact of how much information he has and how he uses that information to develop and manage a project. Project managers are the first to admit that *knowledge is power*, and the more they know about their projects at the beginning stages, the better they can plan. The two key components in planning are to correctly identify what has to be accomplished in work activities to complete a project deliverable, and how to effectively address and manage problems that occur throughout the project lifecycle that could impact budget and schedule.

Project managers are generally tasked with the development of a project management plan, and how the project manager develops this plan largely dictates its success. It is incumbent on the project manager to view the project in a best-case scenario where simply planning all of the activities and resources required to accomplish an objective should be sufficient, but planning for problems is equally as important, given their potential to destroy or delay a project. All too often the project manager gets wrapped up at the beginning of the project in ensuring that all of the normal activities, resources, and purchases are in place but does not leave time to identify and plan responses for potential problems. If the project manager has allocated time to design a project that will be conducted correctly, ensuring a project deliverable is completed on budget and on schedule, it is also the project manager's responsibility to plan for risks and responses that will also ensure the project deliverable is completed on schedule and on budget. The project manager, in planning risk responses and procurement in advance of the project, is actually being proactive in protecting the project from its own resources and activities.

Part I
Risk and Procurement Planning

Project managers spend a great deal of time at the beginning of a project planning various components of a project. This can include the assessment of risk and everything that will need to be purchased, which is called procurement. As the project manager prepares to evaluate risk throughout the project lifecycle, she must plan the details of all the activities to be carried out. This allows her to correctly evaluate and effectively plan for risks on her project, creating what is called the risk management plan. One of the most powerful tools a project manager can have is a plan for problems that could potentially cause a negative effect on work activity.

If the project manager is aware of potential problems at the beginning of a project, he can analyze the probability of the problem occurring and its potential impact on a project deliverable, budget, or schedule, and then he can develop a response intended to reduce or eliminate the risk. If the project manager has a list of potential risks for each work activity and a response for each risk prepared, he can anticipate problems before they happen and reduce or eliminate the impact the risk could have on the work activity. This is like giving the project manager a crystal ball and having the answers to problems before they happen.

The key elements in developing a risk management plan are identifying risks, analyzing risks for their probability of occurrence and potential impact to the project, and planning a response that would be most effective in reducing or eliminating the risk. Developing this plan puts the project manager in a proactive response mode to effectively manage the development of the project deliverable and keep the project on budget and on schedule.

Another important component required on projects is the acquisition of all human resources, materials and supplies, equipment and facilities, and funding necessary to carry out work activities required to accomplish a project objective; this is called procurement. As you will discover throughout this book, there are multiple ways to purchase items and negotiate contracts that can actually be used as a strategy by both the project manager and purchasing agents. As relationships are developed with suppliers, vendors, and subcontractors, there also is risk in conducting transactions. Developing a strategy for procurement can help in reducing risk.

Although project managers typically have the bigger picture in mind and can see where items will need to be purchased throughout the project lifecycle, they can also work with the procurement department to make volume purchases or deals at strategic times throughout the project lifecycle in order to, for example, take advantage of special pricing or delivery conditions that can save either time or money. Procurement presents opportunities for both the project manager and purchasing agents to use strategy to ensure items purchased are correct, are purchased at or below budget, and are delivered on or before they are scheduled.

Project managers should allocate time at the beginning of a project to develop the risk management plan, and time should also be invested in developing a procurement management plan. With regard to planning risk, quality time spent at the beginning of the project is a valuable investment—problems are inevitable throughout the project lifecycle, and being prepared for problems puts the project manager a step ahead in proactively managing the project.

1

Risk Strategy and Planning

1.1 Introduction

All projects, large or small, simple or complex, have the potential for project activities to face changes due to the reality of risk events and their influence. There are two types of events—risks and uncertainties. The project manager must develop a plan to address these types of issues. The first step in addressing risk on projects is to understand that risk events will likely happen to some degree on every project, and a plan for dealing with risk should be developed. The best way the project manager can accomplish this is to change the mindset from worrying about problems that might occur to designing a risk management plan as a process that's carried out on every project.

As with many things that need to happen in the development of a project, such as developing plans for managing schedules, cost, human resources, scope, and stakeholders, a plan for risk should be developed along with all of these. One of the best things a project manager can do to improve his effectiveness is to develop processes for all of the things that must be managed and use these processes as tools on every project, like a project management template. The more these tools (processes) are used, they can be improved and made more effective, allowing the project manager to have more control over how the project is designed and carried out.

When the project manager includes risk management as a process in the development of a project, she changes her way of evaluating risk from that of designing reactive responses to developing a proactive mitigation or elimination plan. The primary difference with this line of thought is to expect risk events to happen and therefore design the project to best mitigate or eliminate risks in the planning stages of the project development.

Practical Application

The concept of proactive planning was developed in the manufacturing environment. During the design review process, manufacturing engineers develop processes for manufacturing a prototype product. Design engineers typically design products for best performance, whereas manufacturing engineers look at the product in terms of potential problems that might occur in the manufacturing of the product or in longevity as a result of design flaws in the functional assembly of the prototype that may result in failures. This created the concept of Design for Manufacturing (DFM). When project managers evaluate the design (development) of a project and look at each activity from a functionality standpoint as a process step, in many cases design flaws can be found, and opportunities to improve an activity can mitigate or even eliminate risk events before the activity starts.

This type of thinking requires the project manager to look at the project through different eyes and think outside the box of how things can go wrong on a project. Proactive risk planning requires understanding the processes within the project well enough to understand how they can go wrong in order to evaluate how they can be modified to mitigate or eliminate risk events. This chapter explores the concept of planning a risk strategy or process, as well as tools and techniques the project manager can employ to not only plan for risk, but also to actually design projects to eliminate risk.

1.2 Risk Strategy Versus Risk Planning

Projects, given their structure of organized activities, have a propensity to attract problems and to change; therefore, project managers need to have a way to address how they will deal with problems on a project. This can sometimes be a confusing phase of project development, as the project manager has to decipher what can be several levels of information that can be used in developing an approach to addressing potential risks. To help avoid confusion, we must first separate and define two major levels of how the project manager approaches problems within a given organizational structure for a specific project—*Risk Strategy* and *Risk Planning*.

In the role of project manager, an individual is in a position to be involved with management level decisions and organizational strategy in addition to working closely with those involved in project work activities. Depending on how the organization is structured, this can put the project manager in a confusing dilemma of what true responsibilities they have within the organization and the importance of understanding what managerial level the position actually holds. In most organizations, higher levels of management focus more on organizational strategy—a global approach to address processes throughout the organization. Lower levels of management deal more in the tactical areas of day-to-day activities and the responsibility of dealing with issues specific to those activities. The project manager must understand what level he is operating at to avoid confusion in understanding his responsibility and whether he is in strategic planning or in a more tactical level of planning for a specific project.

The primary difference between risk and strategic planning is that risk planning has a smaller scope and is used more as a tactical tool for addressing specific types of risks relative to specific project activities. Risk strategy has a larger scope and addresses how the organization is structured and the philosophy of how the organization is designed to address problems and change. Most organizations have some form of strategic plan for risk and change management, and it may be a structured, well thought-out plan or just simply common knowledge passed down through the years. Following are some of the common general areas that might be included at each level. Later in this chapter we cover developing a risk management plan at the tactical level in more detail.

Strategic Risk Planning

Organizations, whether they have projects or not, have to address the reality of risk events happening that will have an impact on the operation in some way, shape, or form. This can be risks seen within the accounting department, engineering department, executive management decisions, as well as manufacturing, shipping and receiving, and sales. Once organizations are established and have been in operation, they have to address risk events and ultimately must decide how to deal with the outcomes. Most organizations do this with a reactive approach, where they will not necessarily have planned for risk events specifically but simply respond to them as they occur.

Senior and executive management ultimately make decisions as to the success of various responses to risk within the organization to assess their position for future risk events. This could be in the form of establishing who in executive level is responsible for managing the response to risk events, what level of risk tolerance the organization is willing to accept, and how risk management is designed and controlled on projects conducted within the organization. This is an important step for executive management, as this does not state how to specifically address a particular risk event, but more the philosophy and how the organization deals with risk events in general. Following are examples of some of the general areas that can be addressed by the organization on more of a strategic level.

- **Organizational structure**—Relative to project management and depending on the size and type of business they are engaged in, organizations align their operation in one of three types of structures:
  - *Functional*—This structure is used to manage projects within functional departments of the organization. Functional managers have authority over resources within the department to be used on departmental activities and special projects. In most cases, functional managers might also assume the role of project manager within their departments. If a project manager is assigned to a special project within a department, he may have little or no authority and is used more as an expediter. In most cases, projects conducted within functional or departmental structures use a "respond as needed" or "reactive" approach to managing risk events because the functional manager does not have time to outline risk planning for projects conducted within his department.

This is unfortunate, as risk events, depending on their severity and impact to a project or department, can have a variety of results in financial loss, time lost by human resources, as well as any impact to equipment or materials that were damaged or must be replaced. This is largely due to the strategic plan of projects being used internally in the form of process development or improvements, or some other function needed within a specific department, and does not require a full scale formalized project management approach.

- *Projectized*—This structure is used in organizations that have projects as their primary business model. This is seen in large-scale manufacturing such as aircraft, large ground transportation, and construction that builds buildings and bridges. These organizations are accustomed to assigning project managers or program managers to oversee these large endeavors, and solid risk planning is commonplace. The project manager commands a high level of authority and responsibility within this structure. In most cases, human resources report directly to the project manager, and he has full control over the development of the project.

  The culture of projectized organizations takes the potential of risk events very seriously and "designs in risk mitigation and elimination" as much as possible to project activities. In some cases specialized risk managers are assigned to projects with the responsibility of risk identification, analysis, and preplanning prior to a project starting, which puts this type of structure into a "proactive planning" mode for optimum effectiveness. This type of organization also realizes maximized profits are a direct result of controlling supply chain, work activity efficiency, and the reduction or elimination of risk events.

- *Matrix*—This type of organization is a hybrid or blend of both the functional and the projectized types of structures, using the strengths of each to improve the use of projects within the organization. This structure still utilizes functional departments but has major projects working independently and utilizing resources from departments for specific

activities on the project. The project manager has authority over the project itself and the scheduling of resources
required for project activities, but in most cases, human
resources still reports directly to their functional managers.

The project manager typically has the responsibility of developing the entire project plan, which includes a risk management plan but does not have the added responsibility of the
human resources piece. In most cases, the project manager
has the opportunity to perform risk assessment prior to the
start of the project, allowing her the benefits of managing
risk in a "proactive planning" mode.

- **Risk tolerance**—This is the fundamental philosophy of how to
  view a potential risk with regard to the threshold of impact that
  is deemed acceptable. Depending on the type of organizational
  structure (functional, projectized, or matrix), project managers usually have a rough order of magnitude idea from senior
  and executive management as to the general approach to taking
  risks within an organization. This might be a philosophy passed
  down through the ranks of management, or this might be from
  lessons learned and a general agreed upon threshold of risk that
  can be accepted on any given project. The term *philosophy of
  risk tolerance* stems from one of three basic human responses
  given the potential of risk:

  - *Averse*—Generally classified as conservative and would have
    a low tolerance for risk impact, this type of person does not
    want to take risks, but plans risk responses accepting out-
    comes that are more certain and predictable. This person
    also avoids taking risks for potential advantage or gain, pre-
    ferring the status quo over potential loss.

  - *Neutral*—Classified as neutral or nominal, this individual
    has a moderate tolerance for risk impact. This person might
    accept small levels of risk but will generally avoid larger risks
    with greater impact.

  - *Seeker*—With a more liberal approach, allowing for risks and
    having a high tolerance for risk impact, this person does not
    have a problem taking risks even with uncertain outcomes
    and is more inclined to take a risk for a particular advantage
    or gain.

Because these types of responses are more a function of the personality of a particular manager or executive, most organizations determine the level of risk tolerance to be used on projects based on the types of projects and the impact of certain risks. The strategic level of risk tolerance is usually the overall approach of upper management or the owners of an organization. The tactical tolerance is that of the project manager, given the type of projects and potential risks.

- **Mitigation or elimination**—This is a higher, more strategic-level approach to how the project manager plans responses to risks on a project. Although some of this approach stems from the risk tolerance type of the project manager, most of this approach is dictated by the type of project. This can be a formal approach dictated by an organization (such as a Project Management Office [PMO]) and encompasses the general philosophy of how the project manager should address planning risks within a particular project and thus be a strategic risk plan.

  Because a project is a unique endeavor to produce an output deliverable and risk events are imminent, the project manager can in general terms make a decision to simply design mitigation for risks identified throughout the project or identify as many redesign opportunities that result in eliminating risks completely. Risk mitigation is a higher tolerance approach of acceptance and simply requires the identification of risk and a plan or contingency for how to deal with the risk. Risk elimination requires the project manager not only to identify risk, but to drive the identified risk elements back to redesigning project activities to eliminate risk. Depending on the type of deliverable, this can be an effective plan to proactively eliminate as many risks in the design of the product and not so much the design of the risk management plan. This is a more conservative, low tolerance approach for the project manager to take to attempt to eliminate as many risks as possible.

- **Develop risk management plans for projects**—Another important component in the strategic plan is to ensure that all projects conducted in the organization have a risk management plan associated with them. If an organization has a culture of risk management, then risk management plans will already be a component of projects no matter what type of structure the organization is operating with. Having a risk management plan may be dependent on the type of organizational structure given it may be difficult for functional managers to produce risk management plans, as this is not a normal component of their responsibility. Projectized and matrix organizations should have risk management plans as part of the overall project management plan process, as risk management will typically be a part of the culture of that structure. If the organization has a PMO, risk management plans are usually a requirement of the project manager; if the organization does not have a PMO, this needs to be a requirement of upper- or executive-level management for project managers.

Tactical Risk Planning

Tactical risk planning is more at the project level and specific to work activities on a particular project. The project manager usually has the responsibility of developing the tactical plan for managing risks. At this level of risk planning, the project manager will take into consideration things like the type of project, identification of specific risks, triggers that may indicate an imminent risk, analysis of specific risks, and response planning. It is appropriate for the project manager to develop the tactical risk plan because he has knowledge of specific work activities and can derive accurate data that will not only help identify potential risks, but how to plan for a specific risk. The elements of risk planning are common on most projects and are general areas of risk planning at the tactical level.

- **Risk for different types of projects**—Two of the biggest concerns in managing risk for any project is the severity of the risk and the potential impact to the project and/or organization. Some of the factors that influence the severity and impact risk can have are the general type of project as well as its size and complexity. From a strategic standpoint, organizations structured for projects might be in a better position to identify and manage risk on projects as a normal part of their business over those that are not structured for projects or do not carry out projects as a normal part of their business. From a tactical standpoint, the type of project can play a role in projects having the probability of a greater number of risks versus an inherently smaller number of risks.

Some projects may be characterized as having a larger number of less severe risks that are easier to manage versus other projects that may have fewer risks with greater severity and potential impact to the project. The size, duration, and complexity of the project can also play an important role in the types of risks and the severity and impact they can have. Large-scale projects might have different risks than small-scale projects, longer duration projects have risks that shorter projects do not have, and simple projects are not subject to some of the risks complex projects can potentially have. All of these factors can influence what information the project manager needs to look for in understanding potential risks and how to plan for risks on a given project.

- **Risk identification**—Another area of planning at the tactical level is the identification of risks. As the project manager gathers specific information on each work activity, this information should yield initial indicators of possible risks. The project manager should also seek advice from subject matter experts as well as previous projects to understand what risks may have a potential of occurring for each specific activity. The project manager then needs to categorize risks and use tools to organize information for each risk event such as a probability of occurrence, impact, and severity as well as contingency planning and assigning owners responsible for the risk event. This again is the job of the project manager to understand this level of detail using tools and techniques that are covered later in this book to help the project manager identify risks, given all the information available for a work activity.

- **Risk trigger planning**—After the project manager has identified risks for a given work activity, he also needs to analyze the information for signs or triggers that he can key in on that will indicate a risk event is eminent. Triggers are an important planning tool, as the project manager can in many cases mitigate and usually eliminate a risk event before it happens. Trigger planning is typically underestimated or not even used at all in most risk management planning, but it can be one of the most powerful tools a project manager can have in a risk management plan.

- **Risk response planning**—The next area the project manager must address is how to respond to each potential risk event. The risk tolerance of the organization and project manager has an influence on how risk response planning is carried out. Depending on whether the risk tolerance is conservative or more liberal (and allowing risk events) determines the approach the project manager will take on any given response and can be classified into four types of responses:

  - *Avoidance*—Identifies the root cause of a risk event and eliminates or alters the conditions of the activity to create a new scenario without the potential risk. This is simply eliminating the risk before it happens and should be the first choice in response to a risk.

  - *Mitigation*—Similar to avoidance in altering the conditions of a work activity such that although it may not be able to completely eliminate the potential risk, it can reduce the impact or probability of its occurrence.

  - *Transference*—Requires the reassignment of responsibility such that the impact of the risk is absorbed by an alternate party. In many cases, a strategic use of a contract can transfer risk and liability to another party.

  - *Acceptance*—The last course of action the project manager should use in planning a response for a potential risk event is simply accepting the outcome of the risk. There may be some conditions given a specific work activity where specifications will not allow any alteration of the conditions to eliminate, mitigate, or transfer the impact of a risk event, and the project must bear the full brunt of the impact from a risk event. This response might be acceptable as a function of risk tolerance, as the specific risk event may have a minimal impact to the project.

- **Risk communication**—Another important general area of tactical planning is developing the process for how information regarding risk events are to be communicated to project staff, management, and others that will need this information. It's the responsibility of the project manager to develop an effective and efficient communication system for managing risk events, as in many cases there may be limited time to conduct planned responses. Information will need to be documented in a form that is clear, concise, and easily understood to conduct risk responses correctly and efficiently. Much of the success of the risk response plan falls on the effective communication of the plan.

1.3 Develop Risk Management Plan (Process)

Project managers can improve their success in managing projects when they develop processes that are carried out on each project. Developing a process requires understanding what goal is to be accomplished, the steps required to complete the goal, and any specialized details that may be required in accomplishing a specific goal. In project management, some of the more commonly used processes or goals would be resource management, schedule management, budget management, risk management, and procurement. The project manager can look at the various aspects of what needs to be managed on a project as goals and develop a process that can be used as a template every time that goal is required.

The advantage of designing a process to manage something is it can be used as a template and every time it is used can be improved on, making the process progressively better. Another advantage to developing a project management process is that it can be used to standardize processes throughout an organization, which then can lead to the creation of a Project Management Office (PMO). This chapter focuses on developing a process to manage risk called the risk management plan. This section outlines some of the more commonly used elements of risk management that can be used as a template in developing a risk management plan.

Risk Identification

One of the foremost areas in the risk management plan is developing a process to accurately identify potential risks within work activities on a project. This is a vital step and should not be taken lightly. This is covered in more detail in Chapter 2, "Identifying Risk." Although the project manager is responsible for developing a risk management plan, she doesn't always have to perform all the actions required within the plan, and she can solicit help from others, such as subject matter experts and those qualified to perform risk identification and analysis. The project manager should prepare a complete and accurate assessment of risk, so it's in the best interest of the project to seek out as many expert individuals as possible to assist in risk identification and analysis.

It's important that the project manager and others who assist in information gathering for identifying risks know the primary goal is to identify as many risks as possible, which includes the smallest impact risk to the obvious larger, more severe risks. The second goal of risk identification is categorizing risks to organize them based on probability of occurrence, severity, and impact to the project. The details of how this is performed and tools and techniques to perform these functions are covered in more detail in Chapter 2.

Define Risk Tolerance

After the project manager has compiled a list and categorized all risks that will need to be evaluated on each work activity, the level of risk tolerance helps determine what course of action the project manager and/or the organization might take. It's important the project manager understand the general level of risk tolerance of the organization so responses can be developed that are consistent with the organization's threshold for risk management. Depending on the size and complexity of a project, this can play an important factor in the success of an organization's managing opportunities in allowing certain risks while protecting organizational interests in mitigating or eliminating other risks. If the project manager is uncertain as to the level of risk tolerance, he should seek out the advice of upper management for the recommended approach.

Risk Analysis

After risks have been identified and categorized, the next major component in developing a risk management plan is to analyze each risk to determine the probability of occurrence and the level of severity or impact the risk could have on the project. The analysis of risks is another very important element in the overall risk plan, and because there is a great deal of information regarding analysis tools and techniques, this is covered in great depth in Chapter 3, "Risk Analysis."

Contingency or Redesign Planning

When risks have been identified and analyzed, a response plan needs to be developed for each potential risk event. There are two general ways to approach risk: developing contingency plans, which include responses such as mitigation, transference, and acceptance; and the redesign approach, which is the avoidance response in eliminating a potential risk. Depending on the type, size, and complexity of a project and the type of potential risk, there is usually a combination of these response plans. This is where the project manager has the opportunity to design risk responses or redesign the conditions of a work activity before the project begins. This section is another very important component of risk planning and is covered in Chapter 5, "Risk Response Strategies."

Risk Monitoring Process

Another step in developing processes within the risk management plan is designing a monitoring system to capture real-time information on project work activities that might indicate a risk event is imminent or, unfortunately, has already begun. The general idea in risk monitoring is to have tools in place that give the project manager real-time data that can be analyzed to ensure work activities are being performed correctly and to assess any initial signs of problems or risk events beginning to happen. Because the project manager will have real-time information to analyze, it is advantageous to determine if certain initial signs could be identified that would indicate a risk event is imminent, called *triggers*. Triggers should be identified for as many risk events as possible, and in the monitoring process, the project manager would then be looking for these initial signs or triggers as a first indicator a risk is imminent, and they would be in position to initiate a risk response as a proactive tool rather than the normal reactive response. This section is covered in further detail in Chapter 7, "Risk Monitoring and Control."

Develop Risk Controls

When processes are developed in the organization, process engineers usually design in some form of controls to ensure the process is carried out correctly. The project manager in developing the risk management process needs to design controls that affect how risk responses in the risk management plan are to be carried out. One example of a risk management control is the development of the risk register, covered in more detail in Chapter 2. The risk register is a document that organizes all the risks by category and includes information critical to each risk event, such as the probability of occurrence, impact, response, and ownership of the risk. This can be communicated to project staff and used to control how risks are to be managed. Another important tool is a change management plan, which can also serve as a risk management tool in controlling how changes are carried out on the project.

Change Management Process

An underestimated area of risk planning within the overall project management plan is addressing change management. Much like planning for risks, changes are inevitable, and when managed correctly have little impact to the overall project, as the change is a formal agreement in the conditions of the project schedule, cost, and the output deliverable. The problem with change is there are certain risks associated with change, and it's vital the project manager understand the importance of following a structured change management plan to avoid costly errors and creating risk events. Change management should be a well-defined process that is healthy. If managed correctly and controlled, this allows the project manager to accommodate customer requests and/or project needs for change.

Closer for Risk Events

Another important area of a risk management plan is to ensure actions carried out with regards to a risk event have been completed correctly and the risk event has closure. No matter what type of risk event has occurred, it is important that all response actions have been carried out, the risk event has run its course, whatever impact to the work activity has been realized, and no further action is required. Even the smallest risk events, if left incomplete, can continue to impact a project work activity and, in some cases, cause more damage than was originally assessed. Unfortunately, closure for risk events is an underestimated component within the risk management plan and can be the reason why some work activities are not as successful as originally planned.

Communicate Risk Event Results

Project managers must understand the importance of effective and efficient communication within all aspects of the project, and this is especially important in communicating the results of risk events. There are two levels of risk event communication:

- **Real-time risk information**—Communicating results of initial impact to project activities as risk events are unfolding.
- **Post risk results**—Communicating the overall outcome of a risk event after it has closed.

Communication protocols for risk event status can also be included in the risk register as to who is to get communication and under what circumstances and in which format the information need to be sent. In some cases, communication is vital during a risk event when individuals identified to assist in the response need information quickly and efficiently to effectively respond to a risk event. In other cases, at the closure of a risk event, the overall impact that was realized needs to be evaluated and communicated to other project staff and/or management. The project manager needs to take communicating risk information seriously, as the reality of how a risk event impacts the project can ultimately affect other areas of the project and the organization.

Lessons Learned

As part of the closure for each risk event, the project manager should try to accurately and completely record all information of each risk event to capture critical data that would be valuable in addressing risk events in the future. Having this information available is how a project manager can design risk responses at the beginning of the project, because she can see how effective responses were carried out with similar risks on other projects. This also serves as a permanent record that shows how the risk was identified, analyzed, and how successful that response was in addressing the actual risk event. This information can also be used if an organization has to deal with legal ramifications of the impact of a risk event, and this information can clarify what actions were taken. Regardless of what the information is used for, ultimately it is valuable for future projects where project managers can reference this information to help in developing future risk management plans.

1.4 Summary

Problems are an inevitable part of project activities, so project managers need to have a plan as to how to address these problems to reduce or eliminate any negative impact they might have on the overall project. Project managers should think of aspects within project management, such as risk management, as processes and therefore not design a unique risk management plan for every project, but simply utilize a risk management plan as a template that can be implemented on every project. The process can also be refined and improved every time it is used, thus making it a progressively more powerful and effective tool.

One important element in developing a risk management plan is that the project manager must understand the overall philosophy the organization has, at a strategic level, for addressing problems. It's important the project manager understand his role at both a strategic level as well as a tactical level in developing a risk management plan. The following areas are some of the key points required at the tactical level in developing a risk management plan and are covered in more detail throughout this book:

- Risk identification
- Risk analysis
- Categorizing risks
- Developing risk responses or contingency plans
- Develop risk monitoring
- Communicate risk results
- Manage closure of risk events

1.5 Review Questions

1. Discuss what is meant by risk strategy.
2. Explain what is meant by risk tolerance.
3. Discuss the difference between strategic and tactical risk planning.
4. Explain the difference between mitigation and elimination of risk.

1.6 Key Terms

Risk strategy

Risk tolerance

Risk management plan

Change control process

Risk planning

Strategic risk planning

Risk mitigation, elimination

Tactical risk planning

Risk identification

Risk communication

1.7 PMBOK Connections (5ᵗʰ Ed.)

11.1 Plan Risk Management

1.8 Case Study (Use for Chapters 1, 2, 3, and 4)

RPO Construction has been hired to build a custom-made executive home in Vancouver, Washington. Two acres of property have been purchased on the banks of the Vancouver Harbor by a retired executive and his wife for the location of their new custom home. The single-family residence will be an 8,500 square feet, two-story structure consisting of wood frame, cement slab foundation, and tile roof. There will be a three-car garage attached, fully landscaped front yard with circle-around driveway, patio, and deck off the rear of the house overlooking the harbor. The deck will include an infinity pool and oversized spa with outdoor kitchen appliances. A dock with a boathouse will be constructed at the water's edge with the patio decking connected by a wood staircase.

Concerns in the house construction consist of pouring the slab foundation during the winter season, difficulty in location of the septic sewer system, and obtaining permits that allow for the creation of a dock and boathouse. The owners of the house have sold their current home and will be closing escrow shortly, requiring them to stay in a hotel temporarily. They have given the construction company the completion date so they can minimize the cost of their hotel stay. The construction company has told the homeowners it will take six months to finish their home if there are no delays due to poor weather, resolving the location of the septic system, and possible delays in obtaining permits. The homeowners have agreed to the schedule. If everything goes as scheduled, the house will be finished on time for the homeowners to move in.

Details of cost are as follows: slab floor $32,000, total risk $9,000; septic sewer system cost $18,800, total risk $5,100; dock and boathouse cost $82,000, total risk is $11,000. Contractor agreed to a late completion penalty of $2,500 per day each day the project extends beyond the completion due date.

1.9 Case Study Questions and Exercise

1. Based on the case study, assess the risk tolerance of the homeowners.

2. Explain how the contractor might plan a risk strategy that would
   address the potential risks identified in the case study.

2

Identifying Risk

2.1 Introduction

One of the most important components in developing a project plan is the identification of potential problems or risks that could have a negative impact on project work activities. Project managers are usually busy developing the project schedule, working on the budget, and trying to allocate appropriate resources, but in the pressure of trying to accomplish those tasks, project risk is usually put as a lower priority—or due to a lack of time, simply not performed at all. This is unfortunate, as problems occur on all projects, and project managers usually find themselves in reactive response mode, performing damage control—rather than being in control mode, having proactively planned for problems and almost expecting them to occur.

The project manager has the capability to plan all of the things that need to be accomplished in developing a project management plan and can utilize other resources to help accomplish some of these planning tasks such as risk management planning. Depending on the size and complexity of a project, project managers can find themselves doing a larger portion of the initial planning work themselves on smaller projects, while on larger projects they may have staff to assist in information gathering and analysis. Project managers also know they are going to be very busy in the development stages of a project, and in many cases, if time is not allocated for even a minimal amount of risk assessment, it is not completed at all.

When little or no risk assessment has been completed on a project, problems must be addressed *after the fact*, and solutions that might have been available to eliminate or mitigate a problem are no longer available once the project is under way, often resulting in more costly responses and fixes. This is unfortunate for the project, as damage control measures are usually more costly and have a greater impact on the project schedule and potentially the quality of the project deliverable. Project managers and upper management who are responsible for establishing some of the project timelines should realize the importance of designing at least a small portion of time for risk identification, analysis, and response planning; it pays off in the long run! Primary components in the identification of risk that are covered in this chapter include

- Information gathering
- Risk identification
- Categorizing risks
- Documenting risk

In the risk identification process, a great deal of time is spent simply gathering information on work activities to understand if potential risks are evident. This is an area where project managers might be able to delegate some of the information gathering to other resources if they are available. On small projects, the project manager might be very busy performing several tasks, and information gathering for risks would be valuable if another resource could perform that task and the project manager could ascertain potential risks and do some basic analysis on the risks that were identified. No matter how large or complex a project is, the project manager must allocate some time or resources in risk identification to be better prepared to control risk.

2.2 Information Gathering

The first step in the identification of risks is the process of gathering and reviewing information of project work activities. At this point, the project manager is not necessarily identifying risks, per se, but rather gathering all the information of a work activity so a complete evaluation of what will be performed might yield areas where potential problems could be evident.

EXAMPLE

In the case where a project manager oversees the construction of a single-family home, he might review the work breakdown structure that takes the primary deliverable and breaks it down into its smallest components, yielding the most detailed information to review. In this case, one of the first steps would be to review the site survey and ground preparation task where the project manager might identify potential problems regarding the company performing the survey, such as their reputation or having adequate experience at identifying boundaries and ground elevation. Other elements might be in relation to the excavation of the ground and problems that might have to be addressed. One area would be the availability of excavation equipment and backup plans if a piece of equipment onsite were to develop a problem and need to be replaced. Weather can also play a role in this initial stage, as well as the availability of human resources qualified to operate the equipment.

This example shows how the project manager, in gathering and reviewing information on the first activity, has already identified several areas where potential problems could arise. It's important the project manager understand that quality time spent reviewing work activity information can yield a surprisingly greater number of potential risk events and probably more than if the project manager simply assumed the obvious risks without looking at the actual activity information.

Who, What, and How

During the information gathering phase in risk planning, there are three important components the project manager must consider: Who will be gathering the information? What information should be gathered? And what sources of information are available and reliable?

- **Resources for gathering information**—One of the most underestimated but vital components of information gathering for project work activities is who will be gathering the information. Depending on the type of organizational structure and the size and type of a project, project managers will have to address who will gather the information that will be vital in determining if risks might be evident. In some cases, the project manager performs this function alone due to the lack of resources or the type of organizational structure where the project manager assumes a great deal of responsibility and is tasked with much of the initial work himself.

In other cases the project manager might have the ability to utilize other resources but must understand who these resources are and if they are qualified to correctly gather work activity information. The project manager might have the opportunity to train a resource on how to gather information, but that resource must understand the level of detail that is required to derive not only the large and more obvious risks, but the medium and even small risks that can still have a potential impact on the project. The person gathering information needs to be looking at mid-level areas of information—not so much the lowest level of detail, but critical areas that may need further evaluation, which might include the examples here:

- Were **specifications interpreted** correctly, maybe misinterpreted?
- Have **critical resources** been correctly identified (capabilities, skillsets, and so on)?
- Are there **enough resources** to complete the activity in the estimated time duration?
- Will **critical equipment** and facilities be available when needed?
- Does the organization **have the technology** to complete the project objective?
- Can **critical shipments** be delayed and for what variety of reasons?
- Are there any **critical material requirements** that could be at risk?
- Is **weather** going to be a consideration?

- **Information that needs to be collected**—The next component of gathering information is to understand what type of information is relevant and needs to be collected for review. The best approach is to take a mid-level view of general components of work activity. The reason being is this puts the emphasis on categories of information that will be under a larger component of work but also points to the requirement of more detail if a potential risk might be evident.

EXAMPLE

In the case of our single-family residence project, the information gathered looking at the first phases of this project—the groundbreaking phase—would locate information categories such as what contractors are used, what equipment will be needed, what scope of work will be accomplished in the specific work activity, the general budget for this work activity, what general time frame the activity has to be completed in, environmental factors to consider, legal or contractual factors, and human resource considerations.

In this example, we are looking at basic information categories because the higher-level category, simply groundbreaking, is too broad of a category to understand any real detail, and driving down to all of the specific individual components is far too much detail and would take too much time for those gathering information to compile. This is why a mid-level categorization of information is useful, given the next step would be to analyze each of these categories for potential risks. Some categories might be accomplished by the project manager, and others might require subject matter experts or others familiar with that work activity to ascertain whether risks might be imminent.

This approach helps to expedite information gathering and does not belabor the information gatherers who can be overwhelmed with detail, but simply points to general areas that need to be evaluated. Once these general categories have been evaluated, there can be a determination as to whether there are severe risks that need to be addressed, moderate risks that need to be noted and planned for, or small risks whose minimal impact might be determined acceptable. This type of evaluation then points the project manager in a direction of what categories will require further assistance in risk analysis.

- **Sources for project activity information**—The final step in gathering information is where the information can actually be found. The project manager should schedule information gathering for potential risks after the project schedule has been derived, the project output deliverable has been broken down into its smallest components, and a work breakdown structure has been created. The work breakdown structure is one of the primary sources of information because it helps separate the information, relative to individual project work activities, into smaller components that can be categorized. The work breakdown structure in most cases does not only have information about specific work activities, but might include initial estimates for resource requirements, activity duration estimates, budgetary estimates for each work activity, as well as the detail of the expected deliverable for each work activity.

Other sources of information relative to the project in general and to specific work activities might include

- Original customer specification
- Project charter
- Project Statement of Work
- Activity information checklists
- Contracts related to project activities, procurements, and/or funding

Information can be gathered from other areas in the organization such as lessons learned documents on previous projects that might have similar activities and the procurements department as to expected purchases and potential problems with cost, availability, and specification of procured items. The assessment of whether activities will be performed indoors or outdoors is important for environmental and weather condition factors and initial assessments of reliable weather information sources. Other sources of information for specific work activities might include subject matter experts, other project managers that have managed similar projects, organizational information archives, and state and local government agencies that would have information pertaining to specific work activities.

The emphasis with regard to sources for information gathering is that the information is reliable and accurate, as it will be used as the primary source of information to derive potential work activity risks.

Activity Information Checklist

The project manager is typically the primary resource who develops the overall project management plan and is also responsible for developing the work breakdown structure, so it is advantageous that the project manager design a process that helps expedite and organize the information gathering process. This can be in the form of an *activity information checklist*. The project manager must break down the primary project objective into its smallest components in order to understand each specific work package or activity, and in doing so, has a great deal of detailed information at her disposal. This information is typically used to understand what resources will be required, the overall duration estimate for each work activity, a budgetary estimate for the work activity, as well as a breakdown of all the specific work that has to be accomplished to complete each work activity. A powerful tool the project manager can use is the activity information checklist that categorizes information for each project work activity and can allow for quick and easy assessment of potential risk. An example of an activity information checklist is shown in Figure 2.1.

The activity information checklist consolidates a large amount of information into a single location for each work activity, enabling the project manager and project staff to quickly assess each work activity. It has enough information to derive potential risks, but not an overwhelming amount of detail that requires an exhaustive amount of time to review. This type of tool is a perfect example of developing a project management process for information gathering that can be utilized in several aspects of developing a project management plan as well as a risk management plan.

Activity Information Checklist	
Project Name:	
Name: (person collecting information)	**Date:**
Title of Work Activity:	
WBS Code:	**Activity Revision:**

Description of Deliverable:	
Required Work Activities:	
1	
2	
3	
4	
Required Materials:	
1	
2	
3	
4	
Required Human Resources:	
1	
2	
3	
4	
Required Equipment/ Facilities:	
1	
2	
3	
4	
Total Cost:	**Total Time Duration:**
Major Risks:	**Predecessor Activities:**
1	1
2	2
3	3

Figure 2.1   Activity Information Checklist

2.3 Identifying the Risks

After the project manager has identified who will be assisting in the information gathering process and has effectively communicated what type of information is required in order to evaluate if there is potential for risks and the sources from where this information can be gathered, it is time to evaluate the information and identify potential risks. It is important the project manager understand this phase of risk identification is vital in being able to spot problems and identify areas in work activity information that would suggest potential problems. Much like the importance of selecting qualified individuals to assist in the information gathering process, it's vitally important to select qualified individuals in the risk identification process as well.

Resources to Help Identify Risks

Identifying potential problems on a project may fall on the project manager, as resources may simply not be available and she must understand the importance of having the ability to identify problems in work activities given the information that has been gathered. In most cases, within the organization there are individuals that might be available to interview specific work activities that are deemed to have a potential for severe risks, and further evaluation may be required to understand the details that will assist in the identification and response planning for a particular risk. Some of the valuable resources, tools, and techniques that can assist in the assessment of information to determine if potential risks exist include

- **Subject matter experts**—Can be used to help analyze work activity information to determine if potential risks might exist. These resources are typically individuals with specific background or experience in the type of work performed on a specific work activity and are able to give advice as to the types of problems that are likely to be associated with that work activity. Subject matter experts are considered to have valuable information, as in most cases their knowledge is based on first-hand experience. This type of knowledge is used not only in assessing potential risks, but can shed light on other details as to the severity and possible impact a risk might have, as well as response solutions. The project manager should seek out any subject matter experts that might be available, as they can provide immediate information that is generally considered accurate and reliable, allowing the project manager to accomplish risk identification effectively and efficiently.

- **Brainstorming**—Is a form of interviewing individuals knowledgeable on the subject matter in a group session where ideas are shared and comments from everyone are evaluated that can generate new ideas as to potential risks, severity, and impact to the project. Brainstorming can be a powerful tool, as it allows for *all* ideas, good or bad, to be put on the table, and in many cases this will spark other ideas that will in turn create new ideas that can yield information about potential risks that might not have been considered yet from the initial activity information evaluation.

- **Delphi method**—Is a simple and commonly used method of identifying potential problems on a project. The Delphi method was developed in 1969 by the RAND Corporation as a group consensus decision-making process. It incorporates the development of a group of subject matter experts (SME), managerial staff, and others internal or external to an organization who would have specific information regarding a project work activity and knowledge of corresponding problems that would be probable—as well as the best solution for that activity. The key element in the success of the Delphi method is the dialog between the panel of experts that results in the reconsideration and narrowing-down process of potential risks to the "most probable risks" based on the consensus (*expert opinion*) of the panel.

- **SWOT**—Is another form of risk identification used in evaluating work activity requirements compared to the plan that will be used to carry out the activities. The goal is to determine if there are inconsistencies or problems in the planning of an activity by evaluating the Strengths, Weaknesses, Opportunities, and Threats commonly referred to as a SWOT analysis. This type of evaluation yields weaknesses and threats in an activity plan that may reveal potential risks. As we know, risks can have both a negative and positive affect, and this analysis reveals strengths and opportunities that may not have been considered in the planning stage.

- **Checklist**—Is a unique tool that is usually developed from subject matter experts, management, and others who have experience with the types of activities carried out on projects within the organization. The checklist is a compilation of related work activity components common to projects that have probable risks and can be organized in several different formats depending on the types of projects and work activities. The checklist can also include triggers to be used to provide pre-warning of risk events and estimated severity and impact of particular problems and successful responses. The checklist works as a living lessons learned document within an organization, specific to projects in the organization that can be periodically updated and used by project managers to expedite risk identification on new projects.

- **Diagramming methods**—As the project manager and other staff assisting in the identification of risks go through information that has been gathered, many risks become evident on the surface evaluation of activity information. Obvious risks are easy to spot, while other risks may be revealed through information from subject matter experts and brainstorming exercises that could shed light on potential problems. Another form of risk identification is further evaluation of activities in relation to other project activities and effects to activities running simultaneously that can reveal risks. In some cases, a particular component of work may not necessarily have a probability of risk by itself, but if one task is combined with a second task, given certain circumstances, risk might exist. This type of risk identification is difficult to see on the surface but is revealed through tools such as diagramming methods. We use three common diagramming methods in both identifying risks and in analyzing risks.

  - *Cause and effect diagram*—Is structured to evaluate all of the related components of work that are required to complete a work activity, noting how specific issues with each component might generate a problem for the work activity, as shown in Figure 2.2. This type of diagramming works best using several participants, such as subject matter experts and others knowledgeable of a particular work activity that, can identify specific issues with each component of that activity.

The cause and effect diagram produces a graphic depiction of various potential risks that might be evident and how some risk areas may influence other areas within the work activity. The benefit is *seeing* how risks might be evident versus trying to deduct risks from simply evaluating the raw data of an activity.

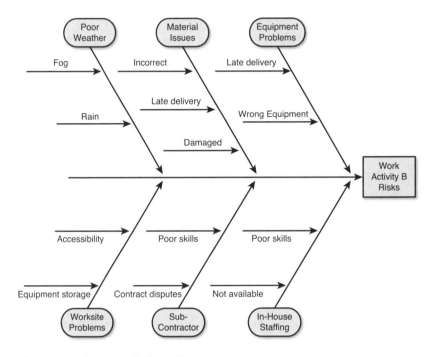

Figure 2.2   Cause and effect diagram

- *Influence diagram*—Is a method of diagramming that evaluates how other components of a given work activity or other internal or external influences of the organization might affect that component of work, creating a potential risk. This type of risk identification also requires individuals knowledgeable on a specific component of work and of any influences to that component of work that could have a potential impact by creating a risk. An example of how an influence diagram would be structured, showing how various aspects of an activity can be affected and can result in other issues, is shown in Figure 2.3.

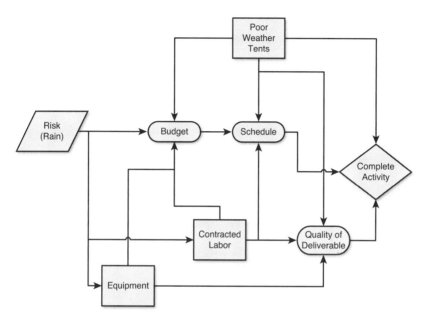

Figure 2.3   Influence diagram

- *Network diagram*—Is used in several areas within project management to accomplish different tasks. Network diagrams are structured such that work activities are connected together within a network, illustrating the flow of work throughout the project lifecycle. One important aspect of a network diagram is the graphical representation of the relationships each work activity has with other work activities and how this can reveal potential problems. Network diagrams are also valuable to reveal if work activities being performed simultaneously will cause problems and if work activities performed in serial will create constraints. Another common area of potential risk is when one activity has several proceeding activities that have to be completed in order for that activity to begin, revealing several risks that could be evident. An example of a network diagram is shown in Figure 2.4.

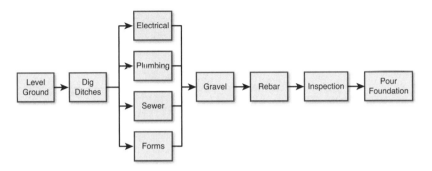

Figure 2.4   Network Diagram

Types of Risks

The next component of identifying risks is to understand the types of risks that help in the analysis of work activity information in correctly categorizing risks. The activity information checklist, project charter, contractual agreements, and statements of work can provide a tremendous amount of information not only with work activities, but with problems that can happen with other areas of the project that may not have a direct connection to work activities. Projects have connections throughout the organization that can involve upper management, procurement, accounting, human resources, and other areas of the organization where problems can influence the progress of a project. Following are some of the general classifications of areas within the project and the organization where potential risks can be found.

- **Specification risk**—Problems associated with requirements the customer has given that define an objective of the project. Although this can sometimes occur internally with smaller projects within an organization, this generally happens more frequently with projects associated with external customer requirements. Some of the challenges that will be faced in effectively communicating with the customer to define specifications can include
  - *Incorrect interpretation*—Generally most common when the receiver of the specification is trying to understand documents, drawings and specification callouts that define the

overall intent of the project deliverable. Although there can be several reasons why this phenomena can happen, including intellectual differences, lack of industry standard terminology, cultural differences, and simple misinterpretation, the focus here is to understand that there is a great potential for error in this particular process. This process is important enough that it would warrant further investigation to ensure the receiver has correctly and accurately interpreted all of the requirements as communicated by the customer.

- *Poor communication*—Another area that can result in problems interpreting specifications. This can usually be seen in two general areas: poorly documented specifications on the customer side that do not lend to understanding the project objective or poor verbal communication in discussions between the organization and the customer. Although these sometimes are connected, there can be occasions when a very well-documented specification is being misinterpreted and problems occur because of poor verbal communications to sort out the details. In other cases, there may be a poorly written document, but verbal communication skills are needed to work out all the details. When evaluating specifications presented by a customer, we must pay attention to the level of communication in both written and verbal form, as this can present a potential for problems and the risk of inaccurately interpreting a specification and producing an incorrect project deliverable.

- *Customer relationship*—In cases of a strained relationship, this can further complicate communication and present challenges in accurately interpreting specifications by the customer in defining a project's deliverable. The project manager should be cognizant of the customer to understand if there are any historical issues between the organization and the customer, as this can create further challenges not in specifications, but in the potential of a risk of the customer intentionally sabotaging communications to have the organization engage in work activity that will ultimately have to be changed. They in some cases create payment problems that can make closing out projects difficult. The customer may return to the organization each time for new projects because of pricing, quality, or because the organization provides changes without question. These types of customers are challenging because the organization wants their business but will have to deal with this type of a relationship and potential risks in return.

- *Documentation error*—Another common area of concern when interpreting specifications from a customer is the simple fact that an error was made on the documentation that, if not identified in the initial evaluation, results in the organization creating an activity deliverable incorrectly. These types of risks are unfortunate, as they were not picked up in the initial evaluation of the documentation and the project was planned with the error in place. This generally leads to the requirement of a change order at some point.

- **Budgetary risk**—Generally a category of risks that can be both at the organizational and project level of potential risk. Funding work activities throughout the organization is typically a hot topic with most accounting departments, and this resides at both the high-level organizational funding of projects and operations, as well as the project level funding of specific work activities throughout the project lifecycle. As the project manager will have little if anything to do with organizational level budget allocations, he is aware that other things in the organization require funding, and although a project was approved, it could run into funding challenges at the organizational level. At the project level, it's important the project manager do their best to provide an accurate and sensible project budget estimate that will assist the accounting department in budgeting correctly for project work activities.

The project manager must also understand that although there can be risks at the organizational level, most of the risks associated with a project budget are typically at the project level and are much more visible to the project manager in the details of work activities. This type of budgetary risk is generally identified in the activity information checklist that includes information about cost estimates for every aspect of each individual work activity. The assessment then would be the magnitude of error of the cost estimate for items in a work activity that may suggest potential risks and not be able to meet budgeted estimates. Some examples of budgetary risks include

- *Lack of funding*—One of the more serious budgetary risks and is simply when financial resources are not available to complete project work. This is typically classified as a high severity risk with a great impact to the project if work activities are either not started on time or will not be completed on time. In some cases, the project manager might not know when funding will be available and could result in extended delays.

  Another form of budgetary risk is cost overruns, when things simply cost more than was originally estimated. Although fault can lie either on the accuracy of the estimate or within an unanticipated increase in a procurement, the evaluation of this risk should lie more in the accuracy of the activity information as to the probability and severity of an overrun.

  When project cost estimating is being performed, a notation in the activity information checklist can indicate if a specific item has been purchased in the past and the estimate is accurate, or it has not been purchased and there is a risk of the item either being more or less expensive than anticipated. This type of information can help the project manager in not only initial cost estimating, but in evaluating cost overrun probabilities.

- *Scheduled Payments*—When the customer has agreed to make payments to the organization to fund particular parts of the project. The risk in this area is obviously the customer not being able to make payments as scheduled, which presents challenges to the organization in funding components of the project as it moves through the project lifecycle. On larger projects where large sums of money are required for specific phases of work activity, these payments can be vital and create scheduling conflicts and resource allocation issues from a lack a funding. Depending on contractual agreements between the organization and the customer and possibly other contractors, there may be a work shutdown clause that requires all work to cease if payments are not delivered on time, which can further complicate progress of the project.

- *Contractual or legal issues*—Another area that is common for potential problems, and although these issues can happen throughout the project lifecycle, they are more probable at the end of the project. Contracts can be drawn between the organization and the customer that will stipulate funding agreements as well as legal ramifications if one side has not performed per the contractual agreement. In many cases, contracts are drawn with subcontractors that will also have funding and legal conditions if one side or the other does not fulfill the terms of the agreement. Contracts and legal issues should always be identified as a potential risk, as there is always potential for conflict with these types of agreements.

- **Project risk**—Types of risks that are more directly related to the project and specific work activity level, and typically have more oversight by the project manager in managing responses. If the project manager is developing the overall project plan and work breakdown structure and has reviewed the activity information checklist, then she will also be one of the individuals closest to each work activity in not only the knowledge of what has to be accomplished, but what can go wrong. Some of the general areas of potential project risk on an activity level include

  - *Poor project planning*—One of the primary reasons project activities have a higher probability of schedule delays and cost overruns is they were doomed for failure from the beginning. Not all project managers are skilled in project planning, breaking down work activities into their smallest components, gathering and organizing activity information, and correctly estimating schedule duration and budgetary costs. It may be the project manager lacks the skills to plan a project correctly or that upper management does not have extra resources to help the project manager correctly plan the project. In some cases, the project manager is the problem, as they think they are much better at planning than they actually are and may cause failure. Poor planning may also be the result of a group effort where the project manager and other resources that were also not qualified collectively created a poor project plan. Regardless of how the project plan was developed, poor planning can be the root cause of why projects are not as successful as they could be, and it can create risks.

- *Lack of leadership*—In many cases, this is the cause of potential problems stemming not from a poorly planned work activity, but simply a poorly executed one. Even the best planned work activities have to be carried out, which include work performed by resources identified for that work activity and good leadership to oversee all the work being performed to ensure it is done correctly, on schedule, and within the budget allocated. The project manager can be included in this leadership risk, as not all project managers are good leaders.

  Some project managers are very organized and can do the analytical work and research in developing a project but lack the skill of actually leading work activities. In some cases, the project manager has assigned individuals to oversee specific work activities, and those individuals lack the skill to correctly carry out that function. In any case, the project manager is responsible for ensuring work activities are carried out as planned, and this can present a potential risk.

- *Schedule conflicts*—Can be at different levels within the organization as well as project activities throughout the project lifecycle. Most schedule conflicts occur when resources committed from other departments are no longer available. For example, if work activities fall behind schedule and critical resources allocated from departments are working on other projects, an activity might not get completed, causing a delay in the next activity, which creates conflicts. Project resources may not always be in the form of human resources, but in the use of a facility, a production line, a laboratory, or various pieces of equipment that are shared throughout the organization on several projects. If multiple projects are in progress within the organization and critical resources are shared across projects, this can increase the risk of schedule conflicts with resource availability.

- *Resource conflicts*—Another form of risk on projects, as human resources may not always see eye to eye or get along, which can present a challenge for resources working to complete a work activity. The risk of having conflicts between individuals can be the lack of work that is accomplished, causing a work activity to fall behind schedule. Another risk is if there are conflicting interpretations of how work activity is to be completed, it can cause the deliverable of a particular work activity to be completed incorrectly. Another form of conflict between resources can be in the form of team dissension where one human resource has several project team members feeling one way while an opposing resource has other team members feeling the opposite, creating a larger problem for the project manager. The project manager must realize that having many individuals working on the same project creates a potential risk of having human resource challenges, issues, and problems. This might be an opportunity to engage in team building techniques that can reduce or eliminate this type of risk.

- **Operations risk**—Risks peripheral to the project work activities associated with departments that are typically supporting projects. This can be in departments performing functions for the project such as accounting, procurement, engineering, and warehouse/shipping and receiving. This can also be in departments that supply human resources required to perform project work activities. Although organizations have resources to offer projects, they may not always be the appropriate or best qualified resource to carry out work activities correctly and efficiently and thus pose a risk to the project. Some of the organizational risk from human resources can include

  - *Lack of resources*—This is the typical risk where the organization simply does not have enough human resources to accommodate all of the work required on a project. This can be in the form of individuals performing work directly on project activities as well as support personnel that are required to perform functions in support of project activities such as accounting, engineering, manufacturing, procurement, management, subject matter experts, and other support personnel. This is another area that can be documented on the activity information checklist as to the availability of qualified human resources for either direct or indirect project work.

- *Technical ability*—In conjunction with resource availability, is considered to be one of the most common risks associated with using internal human resources. In some cases, they simply do not have the abilities or skill sets to perform critical work activities correctly and efficiently. This risk not only results in delaying the completion of a work activity, but can cause cost overruns from rework due to poor quality work. Technical ability of human resources should be one of the categories of value weighted on the activity information checklist, as this can mitigate or eliminate this risk if resources have been identified incorrectly.

- *Managerial constraints*—Can be a risk depending on the organizational structure and individual managerial personalities. As project managers have to answer to upper-level management and other functional managers, these interactions themselves can cause delays and challenges and become risks that the project manager needs to be aware of. These problems are unfortunate, as this in many cases is why organizations either run well and efficiently, with all managers working as a team, or run inefficiently and poorly, having dissension within the management structure. The project manager must simply realize what managers in the organization they will be dealing with and whether or not they might present a risk to the success of the project.

- *Incorrect fit for the organization*—Another area of organizational risk is the selection of projects and the risk a project is simply not a good fit for the organization. This is highly dependent on the project selection process, where the organization's strategic objective will be a key component in approving a project and can play a large role in how successful the project will be. The project manager must realize that when assigned to a new project, it would be in the best interest of the organization that he voices concerns to upper management that he feels a project is not a good fit for the organization. The general assessment of whether the project is one the organization will be capable of completing is one of the most important tasks a project manager can perform at the beginning of a project. If there is any question as to whether or not the project can be completed, this can inherently create any number of potential risks before the project has even started and is why the project selection process is important.

2.4 Categorizing Risks

As the evaluation of activity information reveals potential risks, it's important to take note of details that might be useful in separating the risks into general categories. As we have seen, there can be problems associated with every aspect of a project, but the consequences that characterize what effect risks have can be narrowed down or categorized into general areas such as budget, schedule, and the project deliverable. Categorizing risks should be thought of more as an organizational tool to help the project manager understand what problems could be associated with various aspects of the project and in prioritizing potential risk events and developing responses.

Categorizing risks is not an exact science and can be designed to accomplish different things depending on the type, size, and complexity of a project as well as the types of risk that are identified.

EXAMPLE

A labor-intensive project requiring large numbers of human resources where the risks would be safety, task organization, and scheduling of critical resources—the project not having a rigid delivery schedule also allows for fluctuations in budget, placing the focus of risk on human resources and not as much on budget and schedule.

Another example might be the development of a prototype product where the customer has communicated critical specifications and possibly a strict completion date that may include contractual penalties if not completed correctly. This type of project would have categorizing designed around risks associated to the scope and quality of the product deliverable, as well as schedule constraints.

Although project work activity information can yield a great deal of details characterizing potential risks, categorizing should be a more generalized process of simply grouping like risks together for further evaluation and prioritization. More detail on the analysis and prioritization of risks is covered in Chapter 3, "Risk Analysis." For most projects, basic general categorization can be designed using two primary classifications: the *triple constraint* and *change management*.

The Big Three (Triple Constraint)

Projects are an endeavor to create a unique output deliverable, usually performed one time and defined by a specific start and finish timeline. So projects would inherently have three primary components: an output deliverable (scope/quality), time frame (schedule/time), and budget (cost/resources), commonly referred to in project management as the *Triple Constraint*, shown in Figure 2.5.

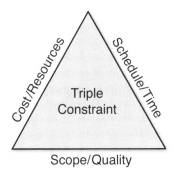

Figure 2.5   Triple Constraint

Each of these three areas are a part of every project, and the project manager should be familiar with each area as a result of having completed the initial steps in project planning. This should include breaking the project deliverable down into it smallest components, organizing work in a work breakdown structure, and information gathering on each work activity to derive cost estimates and activity durations for scheduling. Having this knowledge allows the project manager to see how potential problems can be separated into general categories of scope, schedule, and budget.

- **Scope/quality**—The area that defines the project objective and corresponding output deliverable. The scope clarifies what is intended to be created or produced and sets the boundaries as to *only* what will be accomplished. Risks in scope might include the customer requesting small incremental changes to the deliverable, which creates a phenomenon in project management called *scope creep*. This risk, although creating what the customer wants, can take more time and resources and include added costs that were not originally accounted for.

  Quality defines the value of the deliverable as interpreted by the customer in the general expectations of form, fit, function, and materials used (if applicable). Risks with quality can be in varying interpretations of how the output deliverable will be scrutinized by the customer. Quality can also be in the selection of resources used to perform work activities or services that may lack skill sets, knowledge, or experience that results in an output deliverable but does not meet the expectations of the customer.

- **Schedule/time**—The element of a project dealing with the duration of time it takes to complete a project work activity and the sum total of all project work activity duration that forms the overall project schedule. Schedule is specific to the organization of resources and activities to accomplish a project activity deliverable. An example of risk affecting the schedule would be if resources were not available at a specified time for a work activity, forcing the delay of that activity within the schedule of activities needed complete a specific objective.

Time is more specific to the actual duration to complete a specific work activity. An example of risk affecting time would be if a human resource was not skilled enough to complete the work activity in the schedule time allocated, resulting in an increase in the time it took to complete the work activity.

- **Cost/resources**—An important part of a project that can be affected by risks is the area of costs and resources allocated to the project. Cost and resources are connected, as costs are all monies required to procure human resources, materials, equipment, facilities, external contracted resources, and any permits or licenses required to complete project objectives. Although cost is seen as an equal member of the Triple Constraint, cost overruns are most likely to occur, given that money is the universal tool that can ultimately fix many scheduling and scope/quality problems throughout the project lifecycle. An example of a cost overrun might be in the case where a piece of equipment internal to the organization was allocated for a project activity, but for some reason was not available when required, and to stay on schedule, equipment had to be rented externally to complete the activity.

  As resources can be human as well as all other resources internal or external to the organization, they are typically associated with cost items, as money will usually be required to ensure the correct resources are available when scheduled for a work activity. An example of risk associated with resources might be the original scheduling of a highly skilled human resource to perform a specific work activity, but the resource was unavailable at the time the project needed him, and two lesser skilled resources had to be acquired to complete the same task in the scheduled time frame.

Project managers can use these three general categories (scope/quality, schedule/time, and cost/resources) to design a basic categorizing matrix and separate risks in general terms based on how the risk will affect the project. Qualitative identifiers such as high, medium, and low can provide general assessments of the impact each risk can have in each category. From identified risks categorized into these three general areas, the project manager can see how the project is characterized by which category has the most risks and which have a potential for great impact on the project, as shown in Figure 2.6.

Risk Categorization			
Work Activity	Quality of Deliverable	Budget	Schedule
1.0 Risk A	H	L	L
Risk B	L	M	M
Risk C	L	H	M
Risk D	L	L	H
2.0 Risk A			
Risk B			
Risk C			
Risk D			

Figure 2.6   Risk categorization

When risks have been categorized in general, the project manager can use the Triple Constraint methodology to assess how one risk in a category might affect the other two categories and adjust planning responses to mitigate or eliminate creating problems in trying to solve one problem. This type of categorization also helps the project manager both organize and prioritize all risks associated in that category to evaluate a worst-case scenario accumulation of overruns throughout the project lifecycle. This is also useful in designing risk responses to help reduce or eliminate the accumulation of impact and resulting effects, if any, to other categories.

EXAMPLE

Designing risk responses throughout the project associated with cost might simply be mitigation Band-Aids that can cumulatively have a serious cost overrun in the overall project. This mistake can be avoided when all risk associated with cost are categorized together, allowing the project manager to evaluate what risks should be eliminated, what risks will be accepted, and what risks will be mitigated to minimize the overall accumulation of cost overruns for the project lifecycle and how these responses affect the other two elements of schedule/time and scope/quality.

Creating a general categorization tool not only helps the project manager group risks into like categories, but also helps the project manager design risk responses with the entire project in mind and not individual risks where the project manager can lose perspective of the entire project. Depending on the type of project, the project manager can also add categories in addition to the Triple Constraint, such as managing changes that will be required throughout the project, or possibly a project utilizing a large number of subcontractors and a category specifically to track risk associated with these type of areas.

Change Management

Anyone who has been associated with a project knows change is inevitable and needs to be managed correctly to mitigate or eliminate risk as a function of change. Many times a change management category can be included in categorizing risks, as it can track what changes will occur and what effects the change might have on other categories. In most cases, changes are initiated as a response to a risk event, while in other cases, changes are initiated by a customer to alter some element within the scope of the project deliverable.

It is vitally important project managers have a change management process in place to correctly manage a change requirement. Within a change management process, there are usually monitoring and controls that help in the evaluation, approval, and execution components of managing change that are designed to minimize risk. Adding the change management process as a category helps the project manager in evaluating not only the success of the change in the immediate implementation, but to ensure it does not adversely affect other areas of the project, creating risk events.

2.5 Documenting Risk Information

After the project manager and other project staff have reviewed work activity information and identified and categorized risks, this information must be organized in a form that is quick and easy to use, and communicate to other project staff and stakeholders. Categorizing risks can assist in starting this process, but there is more information that needs evaluated and associated with each risk, and this requires an organized format called a *risk register*.

Risk Register

The risk register is the master template, typically in the form of a spreadsheet that not only allows for risk categorization, but several other critical pieces of information such as probability, severity or impact, triggers, responses, and assigned ownership of each risk event. An example of a simple risk register template is shown in Figure 2.7.

Risk Register											
Risk Priority	Description	Probability	Impact	Risk Trigger	Response Strategy	Contingency Plan	Risk Owner	Event Entry Date	Response Due Date	Actual Response Date	Manager Notes

Figure 2.7   Risk register

The project manager can use the risk register as the master document to record all information regarding risk events, as well as a communication tool. The benefit of the risk register is that it can be modified to include any number of specific pieces of information that the project manager or stakeholders would want tracked for a risk event. This document can also be used by the project manager after the project has been completed in evaluating similar risks on future projects as well as in a lessons learned document for other project managers to review on their projects. Although the risk register is intended as a document that can house most of the information for specific risks, it can be used as a living document, enabling the project manager to make modifications, changes, and additions throughout the project lifecycle.

As a risk event unfolds and the planned response is implemented, a change to the project will be in effect, which might alter other activities, thereby creating new risks, eliminating risks, or requiring how other documented risk\responses should be carried out. The project manager should be mindful of the effects every risk has on the overall project, and the risk register can be updated as each risk responses is carried out. As the project progresses, new risks may be identified and will need to be added to the risk register.

Risk Management Plan

The risk management plan is the overall compilation of processes the project manager will use in managing risks throughout the project lifecycle, which can include important documents such as the risk register. When the risk register has been developed, it can be incorporated into the overall risk management plan as the primary document that will be used in managing specific risks and all information associated with each risk. Given that the risk register is the initial template used to record information for specific risks, it should reside within the project management plan of documents and processes as a living document, as adjustments might need to be made throughout the project lifecycle.

2.6 Summary

The identification of risk associated with work activities during the planning phase of a project is considered one of the most important tasks a project manager can complete. In developing a risk management plan, identifying risks is one of the first processes the project manager will carry out. As we have seen in this chapter, components of risk identification include

- Information gathering
- Identifying risks
- Categorizing and prioritizing risks
- Documenting risk information

The first step the project manager must take is information gathering and deciding who will assist in this process. The project manager should understand the importance information gathering has on proper risk identification and prioritization. It is also important that complete and accurate information be gathered, which can be accomplished using a simple tool identified in this chapter as the *activity information checklist*.

As information is gathered on work activities, it becomes evident potential problems may occur based on certain tasks. The project manager should also remember to think "outside the box," looking at all aspects of not only the work activity, but other activities that may be running simultaneously that may also have an influence to a specific work activity. The project manager should look outside of the project to the rest of the organization and external to the organization for influences that could create potential problems.

Given that several risks will probably be identified, it is important that the project manager develop a process to categorize and prioritize the risks. This gives the project manager and project staff visibility of key risks that have the potential to have a substantial impact on the project. This is also useful in helping develop risk response strategies.

Finally, the project manager should always make it a practice after completing the development of any process within project management to document the work that has been completed. This chapter introduced a tool called the risk register that allows the project manager a single location to document several pieces of information regarding each risk. This is a simple tool that the project manager can use and develop specific to each project that can also be used to communicate certain aspects of risk with the project staff. The risk management plan must also be updated to reflect what has been developed and what was completed in the process of identifying risks.

2.7 Review Questions

1. Discuss the importance of why the process of identifying risks is required in developing a risk management plan.

2. Explain the significance in selecting the correct staff for assisting in information gathering.

3. What types of risks are important to include in the process of identifying risks?

4. Select a diagramming method and explain how it is beneficial in identifying risk.

5. Discuss why it is important to categorize and prioritize risks.

6. Explain why change management is considered to be a risk.

7. Discuss the importance of having a single location, such as the risk register, to record information regarding risks, as well as what categories of information you would include and why.

2.8 Key Terms

Information gathering

Identifying risks

Categorizing risks

Activity information checklist

Change management

Triple Constraint

Risk register

Risk management plan

2.9 PMBOK Connections (5th Ed.)

11.2 Identify Risks

2.10 Case Study Questions (Use Case Study in Chapter 1)

1. Use the activity information checklist to gather information concerning work activities.
2. Based on the information gathered, identify potential risks.
3. Create a basic risk register and record risk information.
4. Categorize risks based on the three main categories of cost, schedule, and quality of deliverable.

3

Risk Analysis

3.1 Introduction

In reviewing work activity information, as the project manager discovers possible risks, a great deal of information will likely be discovered that can be used to characterize, prioritize, and develop a response plan that is needed for each risk. The analysis of information regarding each risk is a critical step in developing a response to each risk and should not be taken lightly. As we learned in Chapter 2, "Identifying Risk," the development of a risk response can in itself create new risks depending on how the response is implemented. Correctly and accurately analyzing information regarding each risk ultimately plays a role in how much the risk will impact the budget of a project and what effects it will have on the project schedule, the allocation of resources, as well as the overall outcome of work activity deliverables.

The study of project activity data specific to potential risks yields information that can be used in four critical aspects of understanding how to manage a risk:

- Probability of occurrence
- Severity or impact
- Prioritization
- Design of response

The ultimate goal in analyzing risk data is to understand the probability of occurrence, the impact to activities, and the prioritization, which is the design of the response required to mitigate or eliminate the risk. Designing the appropriate risk response not only requires addressing a specific risk, but it can be used as a strategic response depending on what the response is designed to accomplish. As we saw in Chapter 2, risk responses have to be designed strategically as part of an entire project and not just the tactical response of an individual risk. Yes, the response will address the immediate need of a risk, but risks and responses can have repercussions that extend beyond an individual risk or work activity.

It might be surprising in some cases what the project manager can accomplish in designing risk responses based on analyzing project activity information and in understanding how each activity fits within the overall project deliverable. In some cases, not responding to a risk at all allows for an opportunity for other parts of the project to be altered, making the overall project deliverable even better, which could not have been anticipated at the beginning of the project but is discovered through the analysis of risk information. In other cases, the analysis of information could reveal that a redesign would be the best course of action and will need to be planned from the very beginning of the project to eliminate the risk. The project manager must realize the critical nature of effectively analyzing project work activity information with regard to risk to correctly categorize and design risk responses in the best interest of the project and not a specific risk.

Another important element in analyzing risk information to correctly designing responses is to be proactive in preparing for risks rather than being reactive and simply responding to risks. In many cases, project managers *reacting* to risks are in a much higher sense of urgency, and in this state the project manager is more likely to make incorrect decisions, or, worse, simply guess at what they are supposed to do in response to risk. In this situation, the project manager can be his own worst enemy by incorrectly responding to a risk or even creating more problems than he is solving. Being proactive and planning risk responses allows the project manager to be in the driver's seat, as they are anticipating problems before they come, much like seeing the warning signs on a highway informing you of problems ahead.

One important area of analyzing risk information is where to acquire good information that allows the project manager to correctly and effectively analyze each risk. We should make the assumption that the project manager, at this point in the project's development, has effectively broken down the project deliverable into it smallest components, developed the work breakdown structure, gathered information specific to each work activity using a tool such as the activity information checklist, and developed a budget of cost estimates and the activity duration estimates. If the project manager has completed these tasks, several sources of accurate and complete data will be available, which can include:

- Project work breakdown structure
- Activity Information Checklist
- Interviews with project staff having direct experience with the work activity
- Interviews with others in the organization having direct experience with a work activity
- Information from other projects within the organization
- Lessons learned documentation
- Information from studies, tests, or design reviews carried out within the organization
- Interviews with suppliers or vendors with critical information
- State and local government agencies that have direct knowledge of a work activity.

If the element of risk analysis seems daunting and intimidating at this point, rest assured that everyone can accomplish this task if given the correct tools. During the identification process, risks are grouped into primary categories such as cost, schedule, and scope or quality of the output deliverable, and further analysis must be done to assess the probability, severity, and impact to the project so risks can be prioritized and responses can be developed. When analyzing work activity information, it is fairly easy to identify two primary types of information: less specific/generalized assessments and very specific numerical and quantifiable data. This allows the project manager the option to choose from two approaches in analyzing risk information that will help simplify this process, called *qualitative* and *quantitative risk analysis*.

Qualitative Analysis

Information gathered on specific risks might be in more generalized terms using less specific descriptors, such as *high*, *medium*, or *low*; *pass* or *fail*; *hot* or *cold*; *good* or *bad*. Although these are descriptive enough for understanding risk, they do not have any numerical value and thus are more subjective in articulating the attributes of a risk. In some cases, this might be all the information that is available to assess risk. Depending on the size and complexity of the project and work activity the risk is associated with, this level of analysis might or might not be suitable.

Some aspects of work activity are simple in nature and do not pose much of a threat to the overall project, so a simple qualitative assessment of risk may be sufficient and no further analysis is required. Other tasks that have to be performed within a work activity might be critical to the project and require more detailed analysis to accurately and specifically define the probability, severity, and impact the risk will have, referred to as quantitative analysis.

On smaller projects, the project manager is typically responsible for gathering and analyzing risk information, and anything that can help expedite the process of risk identification, analysis, and response planning is helpful. The benefit of qualitative analysis is that the information is easy to obtain and the analysis can be performed quickly.

Simple and Fast

The benefit of a qualitative analysis is that subjective assessments can be quickly obtained in reviewing work activity information and can be easily categorized. Project managers, in reviewing information gathered from work activities, must first ascertain the importance of the activity relative to the overall project, as this helps determine if a simplified qualitative assessment of risks is sufficient or if a more quantitative in-depth analysis is required. If it can be determined that qualitative assessment is sufficient, this can help expedite the overall evaluation of risk for that activity. For qualitative risk analysis and prioritization, a basic matrix can be developed to list risk information that can be used to quickly determine which risks need further analysis and which should just be noted that a basic response plan was identified but no further action is required.

Risk Assessment Matrix

The *qualitative risk assessment matrix*, sometimes referred to as a *probability and impact matrix*, can be a simple document to effectively analyze risk. It can be used as a summarizing tool to see how risks compare with each other within certain larger blocks of categorization and how simple and easy prioritization of risks can actually be accomplished. The matrix uses a qualitative assessment of both probability and impact in terms of low, medium, and high. It can also include a weighting factor to help in prioritizing risks. An example of a qualitative risk assessment matrix is shown in Figure 3.1.

Risk Assessment Matrix			
Risk	**Impact**	**Likelihood**	**Sum of Weight**
Shipments delayed	High	High	6
Long lead time (hardware)	High	Med	5
Resources unavailable	Low	High	4
Rework problems	Low	Med	3

Low = 1   Med = 2   High = 3

Figure 3.1 Qualitative risk assessment matrix

As the project manager continues to identify risks where qualitative analysis is appropriate to use for assessment, it might be necessary to understand how the outcome of a risk can change if influenced by other factors within a work activity or other activities on a project. This is an important factor, as in many cases problems are further complicated by activities being performed simultaneously or by other areas within the organization that can influence the probability and severity of a risk. In this case, other forms of qualitative risk assessment can be utilized in risk analysis, such as diagramming methods. Although diagramming methods were used in Chapter 2 for risk identification, they can also be powerful tools used to analyze how risks can be influenced by other risks, other activities, and other organizational influences.

Diagramming Methods

If diagramming methods are used by the project manager and project staff in identifying risks, then these tools will be familiar, and information may already be in place to use these tools for risk analysis. In risk identification, these tools were used where information revealed the potential of a risk. In risk assessment, the same tools and information can now be used to ascertain general levels of risk information, such as probability of occurrence, severity, and impact, as well as ideas for mitigation or elimination responses. These tools often reveal the opportunity to proactively eliminate a risk before the project begins. In most cases, these tools are useful in determining basic qualitative assessments of risks. These tools can be efficient as well as effective if they have already been previously used in risk identification, and, in the case of network diagramming, used to analyze the sequencing of work activities. Three common diagramming methods are listed next.

- **Cause and effect analysis**—Useful in not only identifying but analyzing risks relative to a specific work activity and how the components of that activity cannot only generate a risk, but can offer more information, such as the probability and potential impact each risk can have on the activity as well as the project in general. It can also help determine if further quantitative analysis should be required of a particular risk. An example of deriving information for qualitative risk assessment is shown in Figure 3.2.

- **Influence diagrams**—Also used in risk identification and can be utilized effectively as a qualitative assessment tool. Much like the cause and effect diagram, if it was used in risk identification, information will already be in place and can also be used to assess the general probability and impact each identified risk could have on a work activity or the project in general. The influence diagram is unique as it, by its design, reveals influences and can easily provide a quick assessment for probability and impact for each risk identified.

- **Network diagram analysis**—One of the most powerful tools used by a project manager to identify the effects each work activity has in relation to other activities and the overall project. The network diagram is used not only to graphically illustrate the connections and flow of all work activities on the project, but it can be used to identify and quickly ascertain the impact of certain risks. An example of how the network diagram can be used in risk analysis is shown in Figure 3.3.

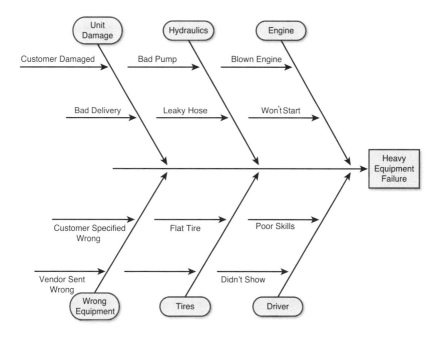

Figure 3.2   Cause and effect diagram for qualitative risk analysis

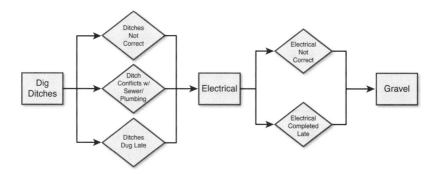

Figure 3.3   Network diagram for qualitative risk analysis

Decision Tree Analysis (Non-numerical)

The decision tree analysis can be used as a simple tool to perform qualitative risk analysis using a non numerical chain-of-events type of approach that can help a project manager assess the impact certain risk events can have on a work activity or the overall project. The decision tree in some cases can be used in conjunction with a work breakdown structure that indicates all the levels of work broken down into their smallest components. The smallest component of work can start the decision tree, and based on the outcome of various risk events can indicate what effect risks have on larger components of a project deliverable. If one direction in risk response is chosen, the decision tree can then go in a direction of response planning that would yield one particular outcome. Going in another direction using alternative risk responses can reveal possible outcomes that are more or less favorable and thus allow the project manager the opportunity to make more informed decisions as to the best response plan for a particular risk. As shown in Figure 3.4, an example of the decision tree analysis would be using non-numerical values to illustrate evaluating levels of probability and impact as well as possible responses.

3.2 Quantitative Analysis

Quantitative risk analysis is much more detailed and objective and usually results in percentages or other numerical values to describe risk assessment. If this level of information is available, it is best to use a quantitative assessment, as it allows for more accurate assessment and effective response planning of budgetary and schedule impact in terms of measurable values. This type of analysis requires different tools that are capable of processing numerical values and output objectively, as well as absolute values describing risk probability, severity, and specific impact. The project manager needs to assess how much time it will take to process this kind of analysis and which risks require the time to perform this level of analysis. If the project manager has the time and resources available, and objective numerical type information is available, quantitative analysis should be performed when possible, as this does provide the most accurate risk assessment.

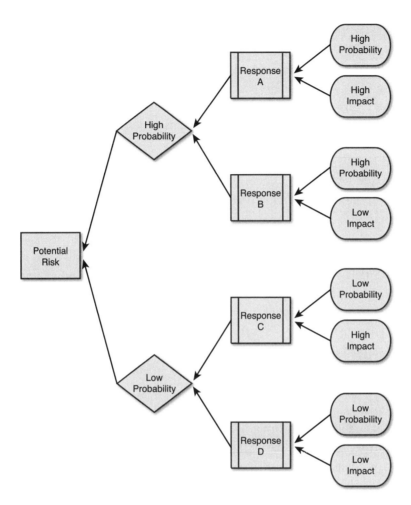

Figure 3.4 Decision tree analysis (non-numerical)

Data Gathering

The most important component of quantitative assessment is the information. Any form of risk assessment is only as good as the information available and the type of tools used to analyze information. It is vitally important the project manager understand that accurate and reliable information is required for effective quantitative analysis. The project manager and others assisting in information gathering, when confronted with more objective and specific numerical data that describes work activity, need to confirm the reliability of the source of information.

If information comes directly from data sheets and documents, they must be evaluated for their age and relevance to the current activity. If information was sourced from individuals, care must be taken to understand who these individuals are and whether this is first-hand information from someone who's considered an expert or second-hand information from someone simply involved on a prior project and who did not have direct involvement with a specific task. Although data sheets can reveal actual numerical values of information, individuals who are experts and have first-hand information can sometimes yield a variety of quantifiable data pertaining to specific work activities that will not be found on data sheets. This can include minor details of potential risks that were not recorded, influences that can alter the probability or severity of a risk, and the success or failure of responses that were attempted on prior risks. Subject matter experts can also help in calculating things like the percentage of probability of occurrence and ratios of impact to schedule or budget that would take the project manager longer to perform and may yield a less accurate assessment.

As quantitative analysis is most preferred in cases where information is available, the warning here to the project manager is that the reliability and accuracy of the information and the tools being used to perform the analysis are critical in producing results that can be used confidently in developing risk responses. The following tools are commonly used for quantitative risk analysis.

Beta and Triangular Probability Distributions

Project managers might find information within work activities that would suggest not only one absolute value, but a range of values that represent a variety of influences that could swing the direction of designing risk response. If this is the case, it is important not to discount the information causing the influences because it might be relevant and important in assessing the magnitude of a risk, which would indicate its severity and impact to the work activity and project. If a range of information is available, the project manager must have a tool to evaluate what influence the range of information could have in the assessment of the risk and possible response planning.

Beta and Triangular probability distributions (also used in Three-Point Estimating or PERT) utilize common formulas in project management where three points of data on a range representing *optimistic*, *pessimistic*, and *most likely* values are used to calculate an *expected value*. Brief descriptions of these values are listed here:

- **Optimistic** (C_o)—This value is based on data that would suggest an absolute best-case scenario condition for a work activity relative to risks. This would represent the lowest level risk severity or impact that the situation might encounter. Based on the categorization of a particular risk, this could represent the lowest cost impact to a budget, the shortest time duration impact on the schedule, or the minimal amount of damage to the project deliverable that could impact quality.

- **Most likely** (C_m)—This value is based on data that would suggest a nominal level of severity and impact to an activity regarding a risk event. This would also be risks having an average effect on an activity or project budget, schedule, or quality of the output deliverable.

- **Pessimistic** (C_p)—This value is based on data that would suggest an absolute worst-case scenario for a work activity relative to risks. The pessimistic value represents the highest degree of probability, severity, and impact a risk could present to a work activity and project.

- **Expected cost** (C_e)—The expected value is the mean of the distribution calculations (shown here) taking into consideration all three classifications of values: *optimistic*, *most likely*, and *pessimistic*. The project manager can use this value as an adjusted estimate for a potential risk that can be a realistic value he can plan responses around. He can make note of the pessimistic extreme, given it is still a possibility, but will not need to plan on that being the only solution or alternative. The following formulas show how the distribution is calculated.

Triangular distribution: $C_e = \dfrac{(C_o + C_m + C_p)}{3}$

Beta distribution (PERT): $C_e = \dfrac{(C_o + 4C_m + C_p)}{6}$

The Beta distribution formula can be applied to risk data affecting something like activity cost, as shown in the following example. Note how the distribution works to skew the expected (C_e) value from the most likely (C_m) in the direction that emphasizes a probability of more positive or negative effect to the original (most likely) value. This distribution can be valuable if information is available to include an optimistic or pessimistic range of influence, to estimate a more accurate impact on something like activity cost.

EXAMPLE

A risk has been identified on a particular work activity that has the following potential impact to increase cost, and the project manager would like to know a more realistic value he could use to plan a response. He uses the following three estimates of potential impact to produce an "expected" value.

Cost increase estimate data: Optimistic = $600, Most likely = $850, Pessimistic = $1,200

$C_e = \dfrac{(600 + 4(850) + 1,200)}{6}$

$C_e = \$866.67$

The beta distribution is similar to the triangular distribution but applies more emphasis to the *most likely* data and de-emphasizes the two extremes (*optimistic* and *pessimistic*), as shown in the formula where C_m has a multiplier of 4 and is divided by a factor of 6 to normalize the magnitude of distribution. This distribution also shifts the mean in the direction with greatest influence. This allows the project manager to take into consideration the influence of the two extremes, but they carry less weight in the overall calculation of the risk affecting the cost estimate.

Sensitivity Analysis

Another tool used in analyzing risk is the *sensitivity analysis*, which studies the impact risks can have on a project. In a given work activity, the project manager might have several identified risks, but to help prioritize these risks based on the relative impact they could have on areas such as quality of the output deliverable, budget, and schedule, the sensitivity analysis helps the project manager prioritize risks. The *tornado diagram* shown in Figure 3.5 is a common graphic to use in sensitivity analysis that not only shows the impact particular risks can have in either a positive or negative way, but in prioritization of risks having the biggest impact at the top of the diagram working down, with risks having lesser degrees of impact. This tool is an easy graphic not only for the project manager to visually understand risk prioritization, but it can also be used to communicate risk assessment to other project staff and/or management in update meetings.

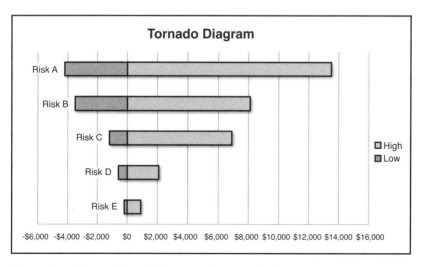

Figure 3.5   Sensitivity analysis using the tornado diagram

Monte Carlo Simulation

When project managers want to calculate the probability of a risk occurring, a popular probability simulation used in project management is called the *Monte Carlo simulation*. This simulation is designed to use information relative to a specific risk that can be characterized over a range of variables that can then be generated using a sensitivity analysis software tool. Limit values must be determined that specify minimum and maximum values used in setting the boundaries or the scope of the analysis. A range of estimates characterizing probability is also needed and can be generated via the triangular distribution tool.

In determining the probability of a risk occurrence, there must be a relative correlation of two or more risk variables that, given a change in one variable, can influence another variable. In software simulations, a correlation coefficient is required to define relationships between variables.

When running a simulation via a software program, it is typical to run a minimum of 500 simulations to ensure an adequate sampling size. In the Monte Carlo simulation, its value is based on the random selection of risk variables throughout the 500 simulation runs, thus generating a statistically accurate probability simulation. The Monte Carlo simulation in evaluating the relationships of several risk variables that may influence the probability of a particular risk can generate a statistical sampling of the probability of a risk occurring based on a particular influence of risk variables.

Decision Tree Analysis (Numerical)

Another form of risk analysis is the *decision tree analysis*, which is a simple tool that can be used to evaluate risk in different ways. With information regarding a particular risk, the decision tree analysis can be used to analyze a range of monetary or schedule impacts that various severities of risk could have. It can also be used to analyze a best case scenario for risk response. As each response may have different values of improvement, the decision tree analysis can evaluate each scenario and derive an Expected Monetary Value (EMV) to better understand the cost of a risk as a function of its probability of occurrence.

The decision tree analysis requires a minimum of two scenarios to be analyzed and can have several included in a single analysis. An example of how a decision tree can be used in the analysis of deciding which risk response would be most appropriate is seen in Figure 3.7. (Data for the decision tree is shown in Figure 3.6.)

EXAMPLE

A project manager assessing possible responses to a risk on a construction project has the following input information: Risk response being evaluated is 75% chance of rain forecasted for a day where the project team is scheduled to pour the foundation of a new custom home. Contractual obligations requiring the foundation to be completed on schedule pose a constraint in simply postponing the pour. Total cost of foundation is $52,350; total risk impact to the project is $22,000.

Option A—Postpone pouring the foundation for two days. Late cancellation fee from the cement company is $3,500; contractor rainy day labor reimbursement fee is $1,800; behind schedule two days, contractual obligation schedule adjustment penalty fee $5,000. Probability of failure or schedule delay 95%.

Option B—Pour as scheduled and rent a large tent to cover project site, rental and set up fee $8,500. Probability of failure or schedule delay 25%.

Option C—Pour as scheduled, provide nothing for rain (hoping that rain will not occur); no added expense ($0.0) will be needed to cover completing the foundation segment of the project. Probability of failure or schedule delay 75%.

Decision Tree Analysis Data							
Response Option	Total Risk Cost	Option Risk Cost	Probability %	Activity Cost	Adjusted Total Activity Cost	Activity Cost based on Probability	Expected Monetary Value (EMV)
A	$22,000	$10,300	0.95	$52,350	$84,650	$80,417.5	$83,550
		$10,300	0.05	$52,350	$62,650	$3,132.5	
B	$22,000	$8,500	0.25	$52,350	$82,850	$20,712.5	$66,350
		$8,500	0.75	$52,350	$60,850	$45,637.5	
C	$22,000	$0	0.75	$52,350	$74,350	$55,762.5	$68,850
		$0	0.25	$52,350	$52,350	$13,087.5	

Figure 3.6   Option data for risk analysis

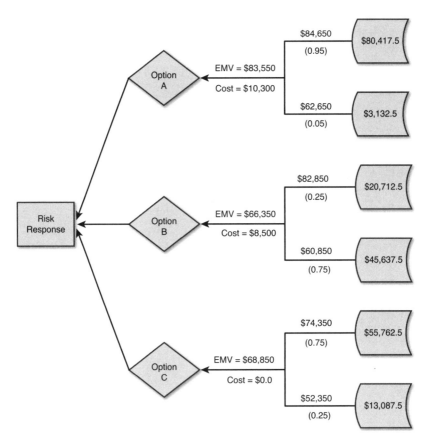

Figure 3.7 Decision tree analysis (Numerical)

3.3 Risk Prioritizing

The primary goal in analyzing risk is to determine a probability of occurrence and the potential impact a given risk can have on the quality of the project deliverable, budget, or schedule. Understanding the probability of occurrence and potential impact of a risk can give the project manager information to prepare responses for particular risks. In some cases at the beginning of a project, understanding the probability of occurrence and the severity of a risk may actually give the project team an opportunity to make slight adjustments in the project plan to avoid certain risks that could have catastrophic consequences to the project. In other cases, the project manager might simply want to see a correlation between certain potential risks and sensitive areas of the project that may be more susceptible to a certain type of risk. In planning a risk response, the project manager needs to know what areas are most sensitive to a particular risk, given that this would be the focus of the response.

What Is Sensitive on the Project?

In our example of pouring the foundation for a custom home, if option B were selected as the best response for rain, there may be certain items in the work activity that are more susceptible to rain damage than others. Rain might not have as drastic effect on the cement trucks driving to the work site as it would for the workers trying to put the final finish on the cement after it's been poured into the footings. More of the focus of the risk response would be on covering the foundation so the workers would be dry while finishing the foundation.

As the project manager evaluates the impact a given risk can have on a work activity, it's important he look at all aspects of that work activity and determine what areas would be most sensitive to risk. This then would be the area in which the project manager should focus the evaluation of risk responses. It might be that most areas within the work activity will not be affected and only one or two areas would need attention. In other cases, it might be determined that everything in the work activity would be affected, and the project manager would have to evaluate that particular risk as having an impact on everything in the work activity and design a response accordingly.

When the project manager understands what is more sensitive to a risk in the work activity, that directs his attention to what type of responses would be required to eliminate or mitigate potential risks. This also helps reduce the cost of responses and the manpower required to implement a response when responses are custom designed to provide appropriate coverage within a work activity.

Separate by Probability and Severity

As the project manager separates identified risks by general categories such as impact to the quality of the deliverable, budget, or schedule, it is also necessary to prioritize risks within each category by probability and severity or impact to the project. In most cases, identifying a probability of occurrence can be stated using a qualitative identifier such as *least likely*, *likely*, or *most likely*. Probability can also be stated using a quantitative identifier such as a percentage.

The project manager needs also to prioritize risk by its severity of impact on each category. The severity is the relative impact the risk can have on a project deliverable, the budget, or the project schedule. Severity can be stated using a qualitative identifier such as low, medium, or high impact, and a quantitative identifier such as a numerical value would rate a potential impact. An example of a simple combined qualitative/quantitative prioritizing of probability of occurrence and impact can be seen in Figure 3.8.

Risk Priority					
Priority by Probability of Occurrence			Quality of Deliverable	Budget	Schedule
High	Risk F	85%	H	H	H
	Risk C	75%	H	M	L
	Risk K	70%	M	M	H
Med	Risk A	50%	M	H	M
	Risk D	45%	M	M	M
	Risk B	40%	M	L	L
Low	Risk E	25%	L	M	M
	Risk G	15%	M	L	L
	Risk H	10%	L	L	L

Impact =   High - H   Med - M   Low - L

Figure 3.8   Prioritizing probability of occurrence and impact of risk

Category Weighting

When quantitative assessment is being used, and numerical values or percentages can be identified as giving a more accurate assessment, there may be the requirement to add a weighting factor on particular risks that are critical within a work activity. This enables the project manager to see a clear delineation between risks and better understand how to prioritize each one. An example of using a weighting factor in quantitative risk prioritization can be seen in Figure 3.9.

Risk Priority by Weights			Quality of Deliverable	Budget	Schedule	Impact Priority
Priority by Probability of Occurrence						
High	Risk F	5	9	8	9	26
	Risk C	5	8	6	4	18
	Risk K	5	5	5	7	17
Med	Risk A	3	6	8	5	19
	Risk D	3	6	6	6	18
	Risk B	3	5	3	3	11
Low	Risk E	1	3	4	4	11
	Risk G	1	4	3	1	8
	Risk H	1	1	2	3	6

Impact =   High - 10   Med - 5   Low - 1
Probability =   High - 5   Med - 3   Low - 1

Figure 3.9   Category weighting in quantitative risk prioritization

3.4 Summary

The next important process in the risk management plan is the analysis of risks that have been identified. After the project manager has completed gathering information and identifying risks, this information must be analyzed to not only determine what type of risks might occur, but the probability of occurrence and potential impact the risk may have on a work activity and the overall project. In some cases, a risk on one work activity may affect other work activities. It is important during the analysis to use all information that has been gathered to understand the full implications of a potential risk as well as the options for designing a response.

As we have seen in this chapter, there are two primary approaches to analyzing risk:

- **Qualitative**—Using non-numerical and more subjective indicators to characterize probability and impact of risks.
- **Quantitative**—Using more objective numerical and measurable data that is more accurate in identifying probability of occurrence and potential impact.

The next important component in analyzing information about risks is to understand how to categorize and prioritize risks. It's important that the project manager understands what general elements the project work activity of a particular risk will have the biggest impact, such as quality of the deliverable, budget, and schedule. As we have seen, risks can have varying levels of severity that lead to varying levels of impact to the project, and the project manager must prioritize risks based on their impact.

The project manager needs to document all of the analysis that was performed on potential risks and any outcomes that were derived that would suggest the categorization, prioritization, and information available to develop risk responses. This is valuable information that can be used not only by the project manager on the immediate project, but future project managers that might have a similar risk on their projects. Properly documenting activities such as analyzing risks can ultimately be one of the most powerful tools a project manager can provide for not only themselves, but also for other project managers in the organization.

3.5 Review Questions

1. Discuss why the process of analyzing risk is included in the risk management plan.
2. If qualitative analysis is more subjective, explain why it is beneficial to use on certain risks or under certain conditions.
3. Select one quantitative analysis tool and explain how it is used and what type of information it would yield.

4. Discuss a technique used in prioritizing risks.

5. Explain what type of information should be documented in the risk management plan relative to analyzing risks.

3.6 Key Terms

Risk analysis

Qualitative risk analysis

Risk prioritization

Risk assessment matrix

Quantitative risk analysis

Risk severity

Probability of occurrence

Risk impact

3.7 PMBOK Connections (5th Ed.)

11.3 Perform Qualitative Risk Analysis

11.4 Perform Quantitative Risk Analysis

3.8 Case Study Questions (Use Case Study in Chapter 1)

1. Develop a risk assessment matrix based on the risks that have been identified in the case study in Chapter 1, "Risk Strategy and Planning."

2. Perform a qualitative and quantitative risk analysis.

3. Prioritize risk based on probability of occurrence and impact on project work activities.

4

Plan Procurement Strategy

4.1 Introduction

Projects, by definition, are an endeavor to create a unique deliverable and therefore require resources, materials, and funding to accomplish an overall objective. Project size and complexity play a large role in what items are required to complete a project objective, and the structure of the organization can also play a role in what resources are available for project activities. One of the primary components of planning and executing a project is the *acquisition of all resources*, including human resources, materials, equipment, and facilities to accomplish a project objective, which is called *conducting procurement*.

Organizations differentiate themselves primarily by business type and size, based on requirements to meet market demands. Organizations also have their own unique DNA based on how the founders of the organization structured the operation to carry out daily work activities to accomplish the strategic objective. This also plays an important role in how the project manager designs and conducts procurement for each individual project, or the *project procurement strategy*.

The project manager is tasked with developing a plan for obtaining everything required to carry out project work activities, and, in doing this, needs to make several decisions in how to best use available organizational resources. This chapter focuses on not only how to determine what resources will be needed from a procurement standpoint, but in developing a strategy on how to best use available resources internal and external to the organization. Because the project manager is responsible for matching work activity requirements to available resources, in some cases he might have more than one option available and want to include the best interest of the project from a cost, schedule, quality, and risk standpoint in his decision. This is when the project manager not only plans procurement, but actually develops a strategy to mitigate risk and optimize cost, schedule, and quality through strategic planning of procurement.

4.2 Project Procurement Requirements

The first step in developing a plan for procurement is to understand the requirements for what has to be obtained to complete each work activity. Depending on the size and complexity of a project and how many resources are available to assist with information gathering, the project manager must ensure quality time is spent understanding the true "requirements" needed in each work activity. This is an important step in project planning, as procurement planning might be performed in tandem with cost estimating, or, in other cases, is simply the planning stage for the procurement process (typically after all estimates have been completed) of what has already been identified as required in each work activity.

Another important element in evaluating procurement requirements are the details of each requirement. This is where project managers can make errors in procurements that do not correctly fulfill all requirements necessary. In some cases, this error is simply an oversight by the project manager, while in other cases a resource available internally meets "most" of the needs but not all. Project managers need to understand the importance of procuring resources that meet *all* requirements, because this is necessary to mitigate or eliminate risk of failure and starts with having accurate and reliable sources of information.

Procurement Information Sources

We first start with sources of information that would be available at this phase in developing a project plan where an evaluation of requirements can be made. The project manager looks at details that would indicate specifications, critical schedule requirements, capability requirements of a particular resource, and whether it would be best to use internal resources or procure external resources, given the associated risks. This information can be located in some of the following areas:

- **Project Charter**—This is one of the first documents to be created at the beginning of a project that can have information pertaining to certain requirements that may be unique to a project deliverable. The project charter is not intended to be a detailed specification document listing details of a project deliverable, but a high-level document that basically outlines the general objective of the project. In some cases, depending on the specifics of a project deliverable, there may be requirements identified by the customer that are critical in nature, or a critical time requirement for delivery or testing of a component that requires special attention of the project manager, and special procurements might have to be evaluated to accommodate this requirement. In many cases, these initial requests and requirements by the customer are outlined in a project charter as being critical and important to them.

- **Customer Specifications**—This is a document or compilation of documents usually issued by the customer that outlines all components of the project deliverable and describes specific details of items critical for the customer. In most cases, the customer specification is used as the primary source of information on the project to develop other project artifacts such as the project charter, activity information checklists, and work breakdown structure. It is critical that the initial project team review this document and clarify with the customer all aspects of the document to ensure it has been interpreted correctly. Much of the information that the project manager uses for procurements will be gathered from the customer specification, and therefore this document needs to be as accurate, detailed, and correctly interpreted as possible.

- **Project statement of work (SOW)**—This is another document to be generated at the beginning of a project, which outlines details of a project deliverable. If the customer does not have detailed specifications, or the project is internal to the organization, such as a process improvement or development of documentation, an SOW document can be created that outlines what has to be accomplished by the project. As the statement of work in many cases acts as a project deliverable specification itself, it is generally used as a primary source of procurement information if a customer specification was not available. The project manager should take caution and ensure that the statement of work has been developed and interpreted correctly to reduce the chance of error in procurements.

- **Work breakdown structure (WBS)**—This document is created based on requirements and the customer specification, or SOW. The work breakdown structure is used to systematically dismantle the project deliverable into its smallest components and organize these components into a logical sequence that allows components to be built and assembled correctly. The project manager uses an activity information checklist to gather all of the specific information of each component of work, which in most cases yields the highest level of detail of each of the smallest components of work, giving the project manager the most accurate view of procurements. In many cases, the project manager uses the WBS as the primary source of information because the activity information checklist also includes estimated costs, schedule details, and specific requirements of resource capability. The activity information checklists also include first assessments of potential risk, which might be valuable in determining specific procurements to mitigate or eliminate an identified risk.

- **Activity information checklist**—This is used after the project manager has gone through the process of breaking down a project deliverable into its smallest components. The project manager or assisting staff uses the activity information checklist to gather as much detailed information as possible specific to each component within each work activity. This includes all details of the work itself, required resources, schedule requirements, and cost estimates, as well as initially identified potential risks.

This information is invaluable to the project manager and project team, given the project management plan is generally built around all of the details derived from these activity information checklists. When the project manager is outlining procurements and special requirements within each work activity, critical pieces of information play an important role in this process. The project manager can also use the activity information checklist to clarify details with the customer to correctly interpret specifications that might not have been as clear in the customer specification or statement of work.

- **Network diagram**—Another tool project managers use after the WBS and activity information checklists have been completed to arrange work activities graphically in sequence and analyze the flow of work throughout the project lifecycle is the *network diagram.* The network diagram uses a box to represent each activity in which it lists the activity title and information such as the duration and available slack time that allows the project manager to see the various options of sequencing activities and how activities form relationships with neighboring activities. This is important because in many cases activities can be done simultaneously or in parallel, and some activities have to be completed before the next activity can start.

  When a network diagram has been completed, the project manager will have more information as to the timing of critical procurements based on activity completion and relationships of activities. In many cases, the network diagram reveals potential risks based on critical sequencing of activities, and procurements can play an important role in mitigating, eliminating, or creating these risks.

- **Bill of materials (BOM)**—This is a document used when a project deliverable has a specific list of items to be used in the creation of that deliverable. The bill of material is typically very detailed, listing the quantity and actual part number or model of every component that must be procured. The BOM can also include specified vendors that an item *must* be purchased through based on specific requirements. It is a valuable document the project manager can use to compare to the work breakdown structure and activity information checklists to ensure all items that need procured have been accounted for.

Special Customer Requirements

All projects produce deliverables that are unique in some way, and customers more often than not have special requirements. If this is the case, the project manager and project staff reviewing the specifications need to take special care in understanding what these requirements are to correctly identify special required procurements.

EXAMPLE

What differentiates a standard track home, where several homes are similar, having minor differentiation, from a custom home where one home is built to the specifications of an individual customer, are unique specifications that have to be identified and interpreted correctly to achieve the objective the customer intended. For instance, a customer may call out specially shaped windows to be used in the front of the house that will have to be custom-made and are not a standard off-the-shelf purchase. The contractor must take special care in identifying exactly what the customer wants in shape, size, fit, and function to avoid ordering the wrong windows. The contractor may have several meetings with the customer to identify particular details and may require the customer communicate directly with the window manufacturer concerning specific details in order to accomplish this procurement correctly.

There are two important issues with the procurement in the example just given: The contractor understands there are specific details the customer wants with the purchase of particular windows that if not met will be unacceptable, and that there is risk in procuring the specialized windows if adequate time was not taken to ensure the contractor understood the customer's detailed requirements. The contractor must realize that customers may have specific requirements and that if these requirements are important to the customer, they need to be taken seriously. The contractor should also realize the risk that they are accepting in procuring customized nonreturnable windows, and if the customer is not pleased they will have to bear the cost of that procurement and reorder windows that are satisfactory. This is when procurements can create risks and add cost to a project if not performed correctly. It is incumbent on the project manager and project staff to review all details of special procurements to mitigate or eliminate as much risk as possible in procurements that will not meet customer requirements and funds expended on those procurements that cannot be recovered. The specialized nature of projects should always have the project manager on the lookout and asking questions as to specific specialized requirements by the customer so details can be reviewed completely and procurements can be made accurately.

Regulatory Requirements

In many cases, project deliverables have requirements that extend beyond the customer requirements and include items that state, local, or federal regulations mandate. These might be simply acquiring a permit for the construction of a building, registration with the FCC of a specialized telecom broadcast product, or the requirement of special materials or products that have to be used within a particular industry. In these cases, the project manager needs to be aware that these are specialized procurements and that they will need to be performed correctly to avoid problems with government regulations and possible inspections. In some cases, a particular industry governs the creation of items or the construction of processing plants and materials that are used, while in other cases the government has imposed regulations that control certain aspects of an industry.

EXAMPLE

A project manager overseeing the creation of a new food processing plan must realize that several areas within his plan have FDA (Food and Drug Administration) stipulations on specific pieces of machinery used in food processing. This might include the type of metal used on storage containers, the types of hoses and tubes used in the transfer of food product from one machine to the next, and other specialized conditions that need to be controlled while processing food for human consumption in the United States.

The project manager in the given example must be aware how food is being created within this food processing plant and must seek advice from subject matter experts as to specific state, local, and federal requirements of machines and processes and all materials used in the creation of the food processing plant to avoid procurement of materials that will not be in compliance. Regulatory requirements should be seen by the project manager as similar to specialized customer requirements. Special care must be taken and understanding gained regarding the specific details of what the requirements are so procurements can be performed correctly.

4.3 Procurement Decision Processes

Once the project manager has acquired customer specifications, an SOW and a work breakdown structure created, and activity information checklists completed, the project manager can then begin the task of evaluating all procurements. There are many types of items that need to be purchased to complete a project that does not only include the materials for an output deliverable, but all resources both human and nonhuman, equipment, facilities, and any external contractors.

When evaluating procurements for project activities, different types of decisions need to be made, such as whether or not to purchase something or simply make an item internally, to use internal resources versus contract external resources, and whether to purchase or rent equipment for specific work activity requirements. These types of decisions are critical because they not only determine how these things are obtained, but also what type of contractual arrangements are required, whether or not the organization has adequate resources, and cost ramifications of internal versus external resources.

These decisions also need to be made in the best interest of the project, the budget, the schedule, and the quality of the output deliverable. The following areas are some of the more prominent areas of procurement decisions that are typically made by the project manager or responsible project staff.

Make or Buy Analysis

After reviewing project work activity information, the project manager then needs to evaluate how to proceed with certain procurements and decisions that need to be made as to what the best course of action would be in the best interest of the project. Some of these decisions include whether to buy materials or manufacture items internally, lease or purchase capital equipment, and the use of internal resources that might be available versus contracting external resources required for project activities. In some cases, these decisions are easy because the project manager knows what is available and can quickly ascertain the availability and level of risk for that decision. In other cases, the project manager might have to investigate what is available in-house, the capabilities and availability of current resources, facilities, or equipment versus procuring these items externally. These are important decisions, as the severity and impact of risk and making an error on these procurements can range anywhere from having minimal impact to the project to having the potential of catastrophic failure. The project manager must use great care in making these decisions.

- **Make or buy**—One of the decisions that must be made in most cases with regard to materials for project activities is the make or buy decision. If the organization has the capability of creating or manufacturing items necessary to fulfill activity requirements, this would be considered a make decision and done internally. If the organization is not capable of producing or manufacturing items required for work activities, the project manager needs to procure these items externally.

  Just because an organization has the capability to create something doesn't necessarily mean they can meet the quality standards, form, fit, and function and can create the material(s) within the time frame required. The project manager must know all of the details regarding the specifications of an item that may be considered a make item to ensure that the organization is capable of fulfilling those requirements. In addition, the project manager must also understand the overall costs associated with that item and schedule requirements for delivery to ensure minimal or no risk is incurred for that activity.

If the organization is not capable of fulfilling quality, cost, and scheduling requirements, the project manager is forced to procure this item externally and will solicit quotes or bids through external resources. Using external resources to create items will also come with its own package of risks, as the project manager will need to accurately convey specifications and details for each item required to ensure the external resource fully understands their responsibility in creating that item.

With either a make or buy decision, the project manager has the responsibility to ensure the item will be available for the work activity, will be correct, and fulfill the requirements to minimize or eliminate any risk regarding that particular item. The project manager must also realize that for every make or buy decision, this evaluation has to be carried out in order to ensure all items required within each work activity throughout the project lifecycle are supplied in the best interest of the project at the highest quality, lowest cost and are delivered as per the required schedule.

EXAMPLE

A project manager working for a high-tech telecom organization is overseeing the creation of a specialized telecom prototype. This new product requires a specialized heat-sink housing that has specific, tight tolerances that have to be maintained. The project manager has to decide whether to make this product in-house or have it produced externally. The project manager, knowing that the organization has an internal machine shop, would have to review the specifications of the housing with the machine shop manager to ascertain the capability of the machine shop correctly producing the product. If it is something the machine shop manager deems is possible, using internal resources would be a cost-effective way to acquire this piece of material.

The project manager would then need to evaluate the level of quality the machine shop is capable of as well as a schedule of when the item would be completed and available for the work activity. If the project manager is convinced internal resources are capable of supplying this item, the make option can be performed internally. If the machine shop manager deems that it may be beyond the capability of internal resources, the project manager needs to look to external resources to create this item in meeting all of the specified requirements, keeping with the delivery schedule, and living with the cost associated with procuring this item externally.

In the scenario in this example, if the item can be made internally, the project manager has, from a risk standpoint, the capability of keeping an eye on the progress and therefore reduces possible risks. Alternatively the creation of the item external to the organization is in the hands of the external contractor, and the project manager has to assume the associated risks of quality and delivery schedule.

- **Lease or own**—When the project manager has to procure equipment or facilities as a requirement of a work activity, this again requires the project manager to evaluate two options in his decision: to lease or to own. As most organizations typically only acquire capital equipment or facilities as a long-term investment based on ongoing necessity of that particular item, the very nature of projects suggest that these items would only be used one time and may help make the decision whether to lease or buy based on that criteria alone. In some organizations, projects that are similar and are conducted on an ongoing basis, where particular pieces of equipment or facilities could be used over and over, the purchase of this item might be in the best interest of the organization. In either case, the project manager must perform an evaluation to ascertain the cost effectiveness of simply leasing or renting an item for the specific use within a work activity, or solicit the council of other management as to the opportunity to purchase an item for the ongoing use of the organization. It is also necessary for the project manager to be cognizant of the project budget and whether or not funds were available for lease or purchase of required equipment and facilities. The project manager must also seek the advice of those involved with the acquisition of capital equipment as to how that equipment would be charged for its specific use within a work activity on their particular project. In the case of an item that is rented, the total amount of that rental would simply be a line item for that work activity budget, whereas the purchase of capital equipment or a facility, although used on the project, would be charged as a capital equipment expenditure by the organization and the duration of its use billed as a segment of its value charged to the project work activity.

EXAMPLE

A project manager overseeing a construction project where heavy equipment is used to prepare a section of ground for construction would be an example of deciding between renting a piece of equipment to complete this task versus purchasing a piece of equipment. If the organization is structured in a way where projects of this nature are typical and this piece of equipment would more likely be used in several applications, the project manager would ask upper management and possibly accounting to be allowed to purchase this item. Although this is a specific piece of equipment used to accomplish this task, it could also be used on other similar projects in the future. If the organization does not typically perform projects of this nature and is simply constructing this facility as a one-time project, the project manager would simply rent this piece of equipment, as the organization would have no use of it for future projects.

- **Internal versus external**—Another decision project managers have to make that involves obtaining resources required for project activities is internal versus external. In most cases, internal versus external refers to the availability of qualified human resources for specific tasks on project work activities.

When project managers are evaluating each work activity for the requirement of human resources, it is important for them to pay attention to the details of what specific skills are required and whether or not individuals within the organization have these skills and would be available to perform the task required.

Evaluating internal resources can many times be a perplexing endeavor because it is difficult to ascertain whether certain individuals have specific skill sets. It is best that the project manager seek the advice of the manager or supervisor overseeing individuals that appear to have the required skills as to the specifics of their skills and if they would be available in the time frame required to perform the tasks within the work activity. The project manager must be diligent to acquire as much information as possible about a prospective resource if she is going to allocate an internal resource for a task to ensure this does not create a problem if that resource does not have the skills required to complete the assigned task.

If the project manager is running into difficulty finding an individual within the organization that has the skill set required, she might have to go external to the organization to contract an individual to perform the task. If this is the case, the project manager must use the same process and caution in understanding all of the details of what is required to correctly perform the task to ensure she has selected the correct individual. This also comes with the risk that an externally contracted individual, being ambitious about acquiring work, overstates his or her skills and will not be able to perform the task required. This is always a risk the project manager has to take, but reviewing past employment and contacting references to confirm abilities and skill sets can help mitigate or eliminate some of this uncertainty and risk.

EXAMPLE

In the case of a project manager overseeing a project where a specialized software package is being developed, the project manager has learned that a key component of software user interface has to be developed and requires a programmer with specialized skills. After the project manager has interviewed the software engineering manager, a consensus forms that although he has individuals with this specific skill set, they are allocated to other projects and will not be available in the timeframe the project manager needs them, and therefore internal resources are not available. The software engineering manager, however, has contracted external individuals on several occasions to fill in for specific tasks within his department and has given the project manager names of individuals with skill sets that have been proven within the organization to be able to perform this task.

This would be a case where the project manager has solicited information from a subject matter expert, the software engineering manager, as to acquiring individuals externally by contract that can perform tasks where skills have been proven first-hand. The project manager can then seek out these individuals for their availability and associated cost for the time required to complete the task.

In the case of this example, the project manager was fortunate that the engineering manager actually had contracted individuals in the past with the specific skills and the project manager was able to fill the resource requirements with greatly reduced risk. On the other hand, because internal resources were not available, external resources command a higher cost, and although unfortunate, this has to be factored into the project budget. In most cases where external contracted resources are required, the project manager should utilize information from subject matter experts within the organization as to the best options for acquiring external contracted resources. This keeps the project manager from guessing and interviewing several individuals trying to ascertain their skill sets. If the project manager has to contract external resources, she should do everything possible to reduce or eliminate the risk of contracting individuals who fall short of the skill sets required.

Purchase Strategies

As we have seen where the project manager actually develops a decision-making process, this can also be seen as a strategy where the project manager coordinates with other departments and projects within the organization to use and allocate internal resources. The project manager acquires these resources considering four primary elements, *quality*, *capability*, *cost*, and *availability*, to meet schedule demands and risk associated with using individuals on a project. As the project manager uses these four elements in the plan to purchase items for use on the project, they will not only be a part of the purchase process, but used as a purchase strategy. The strategic element of this process lies in the balance of what's required in procuring an item and the give-and-take of options that shift cost, availability, and risk of procuring the correct item as well as its quality.

The project manager must understand that it is rare to procure items at the lowest cost; available whenever the project requires them; having all of the required form, fit, and function; and presenting no risk or challenge for the project or work activity. The strategy then becomes evaluating items that the organization purchases for other projects as well that, when purchased at one time, can reduce the cost of that item in the form of volume purchase or consolidated shipping. This would be a strategic purchase in lowering the cost but may require an adjustment in delivery as it is tied to items used elsewhere in the organization.

Another example would be items that are purchased from an approved vendor list where prior testing within the organization has proven the quality and the integrity of the vendor that works to mitigate or eliminate risk, but may command a higher cost. This type of consideration is where the project manager will use strategy on purchases in order to gain advantage in assuring quality in the reduction of risk, knowing that it might increase cost or delay schedule. The project manager can use this strategy to gain whatever advantage is required to accomplish different things throughout the project life-cycle. In some cases, the project manager might be ahead of schedule and can strategically design a procurement that costs time in the schedule, but gains an advantage in cost or quality. In another case, the project manager might be behind schedule but actually under budget and may strategically pay a higher price to expedite an item to put the project back on schedule. The project manager can utilize strategic purchasing to accomplish various things in the project. These types of strategic procurements can be seen in the following areas:

- **Organizational level**—When the procurement department evaluates purchases required throughout the organization and looks for opportunities to consolidate purchases, that allows the possibility to lower the price of purchased items in the cost of shipping. The procurement department generally has information of past purchases and vendors with proven track records to help ensure quality and reduce risk of items being purchased in error. If an organization has a procurement department, the project manager is wise to go through each of the project activity requirements with the purchasing agent to ensure they understand all of the specific details of specialized purchases that may be required. This is extremely important in that the procurement department's responsibility is to purchase items, so they realize they have done this many times year after year, and if a particular line item has a commonly used name, it may be purchased based on the similarity of items procured in the past, and information on any specialized details may not be considered, causing this item to be purchased in error. The project manager must realize he does have the ultimate responsibility to ensure all pertinent information pertaining to items that need to be procured has been accurately and completely conveyed to the procurement department to avoid the risk of errors. The procurements department in an organization can be a powerful and strategic ally for the project manager in accomplishing procurements efficiently and strategically, but he must ensure this process is carried out correctly.

- **Project level**—There are two general aspects of procurements at the project level, which include project manager procurement responsibility and procurement strategy. Larger organizations generally have a procurements department that assumes this responsibility with guidance and oversight of specific purchases by the project manager. With smaller organizations, the project manager might have the responsibility of all purchases required for an individual project and assumes the entire responsibility for all procurements. In either case, the project manager ultimately has the responsibility of procurements, but both scenarios present a certain level of risk.

As we have discussed, the second element at the project level is procurement strategy, which requires the project manager to review the work breakdown structure and possibly a network diagram to evaluate strategic procurements. In this case, the project manager has the ability to design purchases when required based on several items such as the availability of space on the project site for storing procured items, the consolidation of procured items to reduce shipping costs, the consolidation of specially built parts by a single vendor that may charge for setup fees and savings based on volume purchases from specific suppliers, and so on.

- **Preferred supplier/vendor list**—Developed and used by procurement departments and is a compilation of suppliers and vendors the organization has evaluated and approved for several reasons including:
  - Good quality of products from previous orders
  - Reduced cost on special shipping agreements
  - Approved pricing schedules
  - Established relationships that improve sensitive discussions and negotiations

For a quick clarification in terminology, there are two commonly used names associated with organizations that provide products or services to other organizations, which are *suppliers* and *vendors*. As there may be controversy in the exact definition for these two terms, the following examples may help clarify how these terms might be understood in the business world.

- **Suppliers**—Organizations comprised primarily of manufacturers of small piece part and component type products that are sold (or supplied) to larger manufacturers that create a final product. These are also products that would not be typically sold to the general public.

EXAMPLE

Suppliers would be companies that manufacture small component parts used inside of a televisions such as resistors, capacitors, circuit boards, cables, and connectors. The manufacturer of the television purchases all of these components from suppliers and assembles them into a final product.

- **Vendors**—Organizations comprised primarily of distributors and retailers that purchase items from manufacturers to sell (or "vend") to an end user or customer within a particular market. Although vendors are typically distributing products to a general consumer-based market, manufacturers may purchase items occasionally from a vendor to be used on a product.

EXAMPLE

Vendors would be large distribution retailers such as Sears, Best Buy, and Walmart that purchase televisions from a manufacturer for the purpose of selling the product to an end-user market.

The preferred supplier/vendor list is important for the procurement department and for projects because it is a way to reduce risk of things like poor quality and missed scheduled deliveries, and helps the project manager obtain more accurate pricing and commitments to scheduled deliveries. As the project manager is developing the project plan, the reliability of suppliers and vendors becomes an important element of planning each work activity. Most organizations prefer to use a preferred supplier/vendor list, as this narrows down the search of organizations that can supply items required for each work activity, expediting the procurements process and working to mitigate and eliminate risk of poor quality, delays, and difficulties in negotiating contracts.

- **Source selection**—Can be a difficult area for project managers because in most cases project managers do not have the experience and knowledge of individuals working in the procurements department and therefore are less efficient in supplier/vendor source selection. If a preferred supplier/vendor list is being used by the procurements department, source selection is a much easier endeavor, as the organization requires procurements to use preferred suppliers over suppliers they do not know.

In some cases the project manager, in having discussions about specific work activity requirements with subject matter experts, discover a supplier or vendor that may be the best solution but is not included on the organization's preferred supplier/vendor list. The project manager must be aware of why certain organizations are being selected to supply items required for work activities. They may simply have been on a preferred supplier/vendor list, while in other cases an organization that is not on the list might be preferred, as the product is superior and other elements such as cost and schedule are also favorable. It is incumbent on the project manager to make sure organizations that have been selected to supply items required for work activities, whether on a preferred list or not, meet the four basic requirements of procurement:

- *Capable* of meeting all specified requirements
- Cost satisfies *budget* requirements
- Delivery meets *schedule* requirements
- Item meets *quality* standard requirements

If more than one organization can fulfill these four basic critical elements in supplying items required for work activities, then other areas can be evaluated to narrow the search down to the best choice. Some areas might include size and popularity of an organization, what type of warranties and guarantees might be available, conditions that might have to be negotiated in contractual situations, general customer service, and ease of identifying products required. Although many of these items may vary depending on the organization, they can be used to help narrow the decision in selecting a source.

4.4 Contract Strategies

Projects have materials, equipment, and facilities that may have to be procured, and these items, in addition to human resources, in many cases have contracts outlining details of an agreement between two organizations as to how the transaction, delivery of product or service, and payment will be carried out. Project managers must use caution where contracts are concerned, as they are a legal binding document that can have a variety of stipulations that have to be met in order for the terms of the agreement to be fulfilled, which can also introduce risks. This section goes into detail outlining what contracts are, why they are used, several different types of contracts, risks associated with using contracts, and strategies in how contracts can be used to accomplish more than what is called out in the contract terms.

What Is a Contract?

Projects require materials and resources to carry out project work activities that result in the completion of a deliverable that fulfills the project objective. Some organizations have the required materials and resources in-house to complete work activities and do not need to obtain these externally. Depending on what is being purchased and from what source (seller), terms of an agreement for the purchase must be established, and if both parties, "buyer and seller," agree, the purchase is finalized. The basis of this purchase agreement is founded on four basic principles:

1. **Seller** offers a product or service that can be obtained for a particular compensation (establishes a value, cost of goods sold, and profit margin).

2. **Buyer** identifies the product or service offered by a seller as fulfilling a requirement and evaluates a proposed compensation (also establishes a value, budget, and necessity).

3. **Seller** agrees to deliver a product or service for a compensation proposed by the buyer (establishes common ground and agreement).

4. Both **buyer and seller** fulfill the terms of their agreement (transaction is completed).

These four basic principles, surprisingly, are used by nearly everyone in purchasing day-to-day items such as groceries at a grocery store, gasoline at the gas station, tools from a hardware store, and general consumer items at large retail outlet stores.

EXAMPLE

You arrive at a gas station to find a product being offered (gasoline at the pump) at an advertised price. The gas gauge in your vehicle indicates the necessity of more gasoline and therefore requires you to evaluate your budget and the necessity for the amount of gas required. If you agree to purchase an estimated amount of gasoline at the advertised price, you have arrived on an agreement between you and the owner of the gas station. Upon successfully transferring the gasoline from the pump to your vehicle and the successful transfer of funds that will be paid for the gasoline, the buyer and seller have fulfilled the terms of their agreement, and the transaction is completed.

As we can see, the four basic principles apply to purchases in our everyday life and in many cases apply to purchases for products or services required on project activities within an organization. Purchasing things in our day-to-day lives rarely necessitates a formal legal document, so why would legal documents need to be drafted and signed by two parties if the four basic principles apply and would be sufficient to procure products and services from suppliers and vendors for project activity requirements? In actuality, a legal document *is* created for most day-to-day purchases; it's called a receipt, which documents basic details of a transaction (agreement) and can be used to carry out further actions if required by either the seller or the buyer.

A receipt is a simple document that lists basic items of the transaction, such as the name of the seller, time and date of transaction, a summary of what was purchased, and an indication of payment type and amount. In most consumer transactions, there is a return policy that is either on the receipt or posted somewhere in the seller's establishment that indicates if the buyer is not satisfied with his purchase; under certain circumstances he can return the item for replacement or refund. The receipt in some cases helps protect the seller if the buyer is accusing the seller of not supplying the correct product or service or charging a price that was not agreed upon. If a simple receipt can be used to document basic elements of a transaction and a seller has a return policy, why would there need to be any other documents required in transactions carried out for procurements on project activities? The answer lies in one simple term: *risk*!

Considering the purchases that we make in our day-to-day lives, we have the ability to ask for a receipt, but often we don't, and we make these decisions based on the risk of the item we purchased fulfilling our need and meeting our expectations of quality such that we do not anticipate a problem in having to return the item. Even purchases made for project activities can be carried out using the basic agreement and receipt documentation if a high level of confidence of the purchase would suggest a low level of risk at being incorrect and therefore would not constitute any further legal documentation. If more specific details are required for clarification, such as specifications or details concerning a product or service, shipping dates and delivery instructions, details outlining payment structures, and wordage specifying responsibilities or liabilities, a document can be created that includes all information pertinent to a transaction that is deemed necessary by either buyer or seller to manage risk and will be acknowledged by both sides in the form of a signature of acceptance. This legal binding agreement is, of course, called a *contract*.

Why Are Contracts Used?

As we have seen, sellers engage in transactions assessing the risk of products and services they provide being purchased from buyers who may or may not be able to pay what is required, may or may not be pleased with the product, and may want to return it. Buyers engage in transactions also assessing risk of the product not fulfilling its intended use, falling short of quality expectation, or the seller trying to hide some detail that could cause a problem for the buyer. So with any purchase that is made, whether in our day-to-day private lives or on behalf of the organization for items needed for project activities, both buyers and sellers are always assessing risk and in turn evaluating the need for the level of documentation to manage the level of risk in the transaction.

Contract agreements are used to document the requirements of the product or service in detail to help clarify, for both parties, the expectations of what is to be delivered. It is also common, for larger purchases, to clarify details of pricing, shipping or freight charges, responsibilities of permits or regulatory requirements, and terms of payment to be agreed upon by both parties using a legal binding document requiring signatures of both parties. Contracts are used to manage risk of something going wrong in a transaction where one party does not fulfill the terms of the agreement and legal action can be taken to resolve the situation. Although contracts can be used to protect both buyer and seller, care must be taken in how contracts are written and what type of contracts are used in certain situations, as the type of contract can create as big a problem for risk as it is trying to solve.

Contract Types

The basic structure of a contract is simply the compilation of details regarding pertinent pieces of information that either the buyer or seller wants to include so both parties can be in agreement; this document "contract" can vary greatly in size and complexity. Contracts have been used for centuries to manage transaction agreements, and depending on the industry, common contractual statements have been used often enough that industry standard contract templates have been generated that include stipulations commonly included by sellers. In many cases, contract templates have had legal services draft the statements correctly to avoid legal loopholes in the language. In most cases however, the seller (contractors, suppliers, and vendors) use contracts to protect their own interests, and the statements reflect what the seller wants to protect in the transaction.

Depending on the type of industry and how the seller or buyer wants to manage risk in the agreement, there are three primary categories of how contracts can be structured: fixed price, cost reimbursable, and time and material.

- **Fixed price contracts**—Structured in such a way that a fixed total price is established for a product or service outlined in the contract. In this type of contract the seller needs to calculate all of the time, resources, and materials required to fulfill the requirements of a deliverable outlined in the contract as well as any profit margins and risk contingency monies that would normally be factored in to establish a single fixed price. The seller is then obligated to perform all the duties outlined in the contract for the fixed price regardless of any inaccuracies in the seller's estimates. In this situation, the buyer is at an advantage in that he obtains the product or service at a fixed price under the terms of the contract and can factor both the cost and schedule of this procurement into a project plan.

  There can also be add-on items for fixed-price contracts such as incentives to exceed a contractual objective, for example, early delivery, higher-quality, added technical features, or anything that can be measured and included as an incentivized item in the contract. As some contracts may extend for long periods of time, fluctuations in the economy can change the value of money and therefore the value of compensation within a contract, and economic adjustments might have to be factored in to ensure compensation value is maintained.

  - *Firm Fixed Price Contract (FFP)*—Common in most industries where the seller (contractor, supplier, or vendor) establishes one single fixed price for all goods and services outlined in a contract. The seller is obligated under the contract to fulfill the objective of the contract and assumes the risk for any added cost of resources and materials, and penalties outlined in the contract for missing schedule delivery dates. The buyer must also manage any change requests through a change order process and is responsible for any added cost or delay in schedule as a result of change orders initiated by the buyer. This contract favors the buyer and shifts most risk to the seller.

  - *Fixed Price Incentive Fee Contract (FPIF)*—Also a commonly used contract in industries where the seller is willing to negotiate special terms within a fixed price contract that allows for an incentive for early completion, added features, or anything that can be identified, measured, and an incentive established within the contract to reward this type of performance. It is also common for there to be penalties included in these types of contracts for late completion, insufficient features, or any measurable part of the deliverable that a financial penalty can be assessed and documented within the contract.

- *Fixed Price with Economic Price Adjustment Contracts (FP-EPA)*—A contract used on long-duration projects where the benefit of a fixed price for a deliverable is still desired, but the value of compensation will decrease as the time value of money decreases over time. An economic adjustment, typically based on a financial market index, is allowed to adjust the value of compensation over time, ensuring the seller is being correctly compensated for products or services rendered.

- **Cost-reimbursable contracts**—Cost reimbursable contracts are used when the seller wants to be reimbursed for any actual costs incurred in fulfilling the obligations of the contract objective. This type of contract can also include incentive fees and award fees as add-ons for measurable performance. Sellers typically use this type of contract when the product or service has large sums of financial outlay and the seller wants to manage cash flow and be reimbursed immediately. There may be conditions where the seller may not have accurate enough information on critical purchases or special orders and will not want to commit to a fixed price, as the risk is too high for the seller to cover any errors in cost estimating.

  - *Cost Plus Fixed Fee Contracts (CPFF)*—Used when the seller wants to be paid on completed portions of contract work. There are two components to this contract: The first is a reimbursement of actual costs incurred by the seller; the second is a fee paid based on completion of work and is derived either through a percentage of work completed or a schedule of payments listed in the contract. Although this contract does allow for the reimbursement of items purchased, there is still a fixed fee negotiated for the remainder of the contract, which typically includes the contractor's time, expenses, and profit margin. This fixed fee can be broken up into segments that can be paid out as portions of the contract are completed. This contract shifts some risk to the seller but favors the buyer.

- *Cost Plus Incentive Fee Contracts (CPIF)*—Also used where the seller wants to be paid on completed portions of work where the seller is reimbursed for actual costs incurred. This contract includes a negotiated incentive fee that is available if the seller achieves certain performance goals. These contracts are used when the seller has the opportunity to take advantage of cost savings and the savings can be split between buyer and seller to a pre-negotiated ratio benefiting both sides. This contract shifts more risk to the seller and favors the buyer.

- *Cost Plus Award Fee Contracts (CPAF)*—Also used where the seller wants to be paid on completed portions of work where the seller is reimbursed for actual costs incurred. This contract includes fees that are awarded to the seller based on satisfactory completion of work. This can be a subjective grading process and usually requires a table in the contract outlining how the grading process is to be carried out. This contract shifts more risk to the seller and favors the buyer.

- **Time and Material Contracts (T&M)**—Allows for the seller to be reimbursed for cost incurred on materials and requires the buyer to pay a pre-negotiated rate for time incurred in completing the contract objective. The subcontractors simply keep track of all time worked and bill the buyer as materials are being purchased. Contractors prefer this type of contract, as it shifts most of the risk to the buyer, allowing the seller full reimbursement on materials and a seemingly open-ended schedule for completion. In most cases, a timeframe is negotiated between the buyer and seller for completion of the contract objective, but if the contractor determines more work is required, this can easily be added, as time is invoiced as incurred. This type of contract favors the seller and shifts more risk to the buyer.

4.5 Risk Considerations

As the project manager works with the procurement department to outline all required purchases and contracts, he must also determine associated risks with each item and develop a response strategy appropriate for each risk. As many things can go wrong with the purchase of items and how contracts are negotiated and carried out, the project manager must be aware that risk planning is considered a strategy used in planning procurement. An important consideration in developing a risk strategy is to understand the position of both the buyer and seller, what is to be gained or forfeited in a risk response, and what liability will be assumed by both parties. The project manager, those on the project staff, and individuals working in the procurement department must understand that conducting procurements is introducing risk to the project. As long as there is a buyer and seller involved in a transaction, both sides have something to gain and something to lose and assume a certain threshold of risk to accomplish a transaction.

Buyer Versus Seller

When transactions are initiated, there is a certain amount of risk assumed by both the buyer and seller in trying to accomplish everything required of the transaction. The buyer is taking a risk that in paying a seller for an item, the seller will in fact ship the item requested and the transaction has met the expectations of the buyer. Throughout the transaction process, several things can go wrong that can put the buyer at risk:

- Seller not sending anything and stealing the money.
- Seller sending the wrong item.
- Seller promising delivery of an item on a certain date knowing full well that he would not have received the sale if he told the truth: that he is unable to provide the item until a much later date.

Suppliers and vendors (seller) have an equally stressful time during a transaction in not only trying to market their products hoping that customers will be interested in purchasing, but in other issues including:

- Buyers having challenges in correctly identifying what it is they want.
- Buyers developing issues with payments.
- Buyers blaming the seller for items that are damaged upon receipt.
- Buyers simply wanting to return items that were incorrectly purchased.

As long as transactions have to be made to acquire items for project work activities, there is a buyer-seller relationship established to conduct these transactions and therefore a level of risk that is assumed by each side. The question is what strategy is used by the purchasing agent and/or contract negotiator to reduce the amount of risk for the buyer in acquiring items or resources needed for project work activities. Sometimes the strategy may simply be good communication in either verbal or written form that can reduce risk of uncertainty in a transaction. In the case of contracts, the type of contract used, as well as terms and conditions that can be included in the contract, can help reduce risk for the buyer. The important element in conducting procurement is to understand that risk is involved and that the object is to reduce or eliminate as much risk as possible.

Organizational Versus Project Level

As we have seen in this chapter, procurements can affect the organization as well as the project in how they are conducted, the skill of those conducting procurement, and any liability assumed by the organization in negotiated agreements. Most risk assumed at the organizational level will typically revolve around large payment requirements for suppliers or vendors and any legal entanglements due to contract agreements. Depending on the size and complexity of some projects, just the simple purchase of items required for work activities can go into the hundreds of thousands (if not millions) of dollars, and cash flow must be evaluated by those at the organizational level to ensure funding is available. In cases where contracts have been negotiated, legal obligations are made, and if legal action is taken against the organization, legal representation must be retained to resolve contract disputes. This is why it's important to have experienced contract negotiators review contracts to assess what legal obligations the organization is agreeing to.

The project level risk assessment generally deals with specific items required for work activities. Conducting procurements at the project level would put work activities at risk in having incorrect materials or supplies or contracting individuals that may not produce the work as expected. The project manager has much more control of risk at the project level as there has already been a risk assessment performed for specific elements within each work activity. Risk at the project level in many cases may actually be in better hands, as individual risks have been identified and responses have been designed in case they occur. Risks at the organizational level may not necessarily have been identified, and responses designed as these are generally seen as too big for the project to be concerned about. This is the warning for project managers: that in developing a risk management plan, risks at both the project and organizational level related to the project should always be considered and responses planned. This is how the project manager can protect both the project and the organization from risk associated with a given project.

Triple Constraint

Project managers spend most of their time overseeing work activities to ensure the quality of work performed meets the expectation of the customer, and work activities are completed on budget and on schedule. As we have seen, the *triple constraint* being comprised of the project deliverable (scope/quality), budget for all items procured (cost/resources) and the duration required to complete work activities (time/schedule), is the ultimate arena for all potential risks that may occur throughout the project lifecycle. Part of developing risk responses for procurements is the assessment of the impact risks can have on the project deliverable and schedule. As procurements are part of the triple constraint, they also need to be considered in the strategy of developing risk responses, should problems occur in conducting procurement. This is where the project manager must use all resources available, as well as creative ingenuity and imagination, to develop the most effective responses to risks associated with procurement. The triple constraint is ultimately the primary tool the project manager uses in not only the assessment of risk, but in conducting and controlling procurement.

4.6 Summary

Most organizations have a requirement to purchase items or use contracts in the course of day-to-day operations, which is generally referred to as conducting procurement. As we have seen in this chapter, conducting procurement for projects can include obtaining human resources, materials and supplies, equipment and facilities, and financing required to fund work activities. Purchasing agents and those responsible for negotiating contracts have two primary functions in conducting procurement:

- Purchase strategies
- Contract strategies

We have seen that there can be a wide variety of items that need to be purchased, and there is actually a strategy that can be developed in how and when to purchase items that will not only be correct, but can actually benefit the project budget and schedule and may have benefits within the rest of the organization. Purchasing agents will need to take into consideration items such as:

- Correct information for the item to be purchased
- Equitable pricing
- Commitments to shipping and delivery
- Payment arrangements
- Assessing if good communication was established between the buyer and seller

The second area typical in conducting procurements is that of using contracts to manage obtaining external resources. As we have seen in this chapter, there are a variety of strategies that can be used with various types of contracts and terms and conditions that can be included in a contract to control what each side is responsible for, as well as liability assumed by each side. As we have also seen, there is a certain level of risk associated with using contracts, and the project manager must work closely with individuals in the procurement department to understand what level of risk will be assumed on any given contract. Contracts are also useful in identifying specific schedules and costs that are associated with the work completed. The project manager can use these figures during the estimating process at the beginning of a project.

Contracts are a legally binding agreement between the buyer and seller. It is very important the organization have an individual skilled and experienced in contract negotiation to carry out, or at least oversee, the development of contract agreements. In as much as contracts can be a useful tool on projects and within the organization, they can also pose great risk of liability if not correctly managed.

The very act of conducting procurement involves two parties— buyer and seller—and inevitably introduces risk as a function of procurement. Whether items are purchased or contracts are used, there is always a risk of misunderstanding, disputes, or any other issues that can arise between two parties that would introduce a potential for risk. The project manager must work closely with those in the procurement department to understand all items that need to be purchased and contracts that need to be issued to include these items as risks that have been identified in each work activity. If the project manager is aware of what risks are associated with conducting procurement, responses can be developed in advance that will help reduce or eliminate certain risk.

4.7 Review Questions

1. Discuss the scope of conducting procurement for a project.
2. What are the primary components of a purchase? Explain how strategy can be used on one component.

3. Explain what type of contract shifts risk more to the buyer rather than the seller and why a certain type of contract would be considered on a project.

4. Explain the general idea of why risk would be associated with conducting procurement.

4.8 Key Terms

Project procurement requirements

Contract strategy

Purchase strategy

Procurement decision process

Make or buy analysis

Triple constraint

Work breakdown structure (WBS)

Network diagram

Project charter

Activity information checklist

Project statement of work (SOW)

4.9 PMBOK Connecvtions (5th Ed.)

12.1 Plan Procurement Management

4.10 Case Study Questions (Use the Case Study in Chapter 1)

1. Develop a list of procurement requirements based on the project in the case study in Chapter 1, "Risk Strategy and Planning."

2. Identify what items will be purchased and what items may need to be contracted.

3. How can a contract strategy be used in this situation?

Part II
Project Execution

After the project manager develops the risk management plan and the procurement management plan, it is time to execute the activities that have been designed in each plan, respectively. At this point, the project is underway and the project manager has documentation outlining identified risks and an analysis that suggests the probability of the risks' occurrence and their potential impact to the project. The project manager must also have a plan for conducting procurement that outlines how purchasing and contracting will be conducted throughout the project lifecycle.

When risks have been identified and analyzed, responses need to be designed to mitigate or eliminate risk. The project manager and any staff assisting in analyzing risks might come to the conclusion that some risks can have more than one appropriate response and will need to determine the best course of action. Analyzing what type of response would be most appropriate is called *risk response strategy*. Using strategy to design responses for a potential risk is important because the project manager might find that two or more responses are actually planned depending on certain conditions in the work activity. For example, one response might be designed for minimal impact to the project deliverable and schedule but significantly impacts the budget. Another response might not impact the budget at all but impacts the schedule. Ultimately, the response chosen will depend on how the project is going and whether, at that time, the project manager has more flexibility with the budget or the schedule.

Using risk response strategy is important because it gives the project manager options not only to address the risk but to also determine what part of the project it might affect.

Conducting procurements is similar to designing risk response strategies, in that purchasing items and negotiating contracts can be done in different ways depending on what's being purchased and what type of contract is being used. The procurement department should be familiar with the use of strategy in making volume purchases (to save money) or in the timing of purchases (to take advantage of con-solidated shipping, which reduces cost). The project manager can work with purchasing agents to develop the *procurement strategy* to take advantage of lowering project cost or bringing items in ahead of schedule.

As the project manager begins work activities on the project, it's important a risk response strategy and procurement strategy are in place to take advantage of every opportunity throughout the project lifecycle. It is incumbent on the project manager to spend time at the beginning of the project to ensure risk response and procurement strategies are developed properly, as this type of planning will usually pay dividends throughout the project lifecycle in assuring quality of the project deliverables within budget and on schedule.

5

Risk Response Strategies

5.1 Introduction

During the execution phase of the project, when work activities are underway, is when problems are most likely to occur and the project manager or project staff must respond. As we have seen in previous chapters, the best course of action for responding to problems is having anticipated problems and documented their planned responses. The execution phase of the project can be a busy and stressful time for the project manager and project staff, but spending quality time identifying and planning responses for risk will prove valuable.

The execution phase is when work activities are being completed, so the project manager and project staff should be on high alert anticipating identified risks and insuring work activities are being carried out correctly to reduce the chance of problems occurring. It's important the project manager understand that although a risk was identified and a proper response was planned, circumstances can change, and a very different response may be more appropriate. In some cases, a risk event occurred, but with slightly different details than anticipated, and other response solutions may be available that could present opportunities for different outcomes. This is called *response strategy*. Surprisingly, in many cases, the project manager may have more than one option available in response to a problem, allowing the project manager to not only consider multiple outcomes, but how each outcome will affect the quality of the deliverable, the schedule, and the budget.

5.2 Strategy in Risk Response

When planning any type of activity, whether in our private lives or professionally in the case of a project, it's generally nice to have options available as to how certain components of work can be accomplished. Some people like the aspect of options to individualize some component of work to make it their own, while others may see various options as easier, more cost effective, or timelier. In any case, options give us the ability to choose a course of action that best suits our needs and to bring about our desired outcome.

When the project manager is faced with multiple options for response to a risk, she should take into consideration how each response might affect other aspects of the work activity and project in general. Although this can add another level of complexity in designing risk responses, it gives the opportunity for the project manager to actually use strategy in what she would be accomplishing with a particular risk event. In some cases, the project manager might design multiple responses, depending on certain details of how the risk would play out or a best option based on conditions of how the response might affect other activities. How well prepared the project manager and project staff are in identifying risks for a project determines what kind of *response mode* the project manager needs to operate within and what options, if any, are available. There are two primary response modes the project managers can operate under: *reactive* or *proactive*.

Reactive Response Mode

If a lack of time or resources does not allow for proper risk identification and planning, unexpected problems will force the project manager into a *reactive mode* of risk response. This is unfortunate, as reactive risk responses typically do not give the project manager and project staff time to think through the best options. This type of response will usually force a quick decision that results in either higher cost, schedule delays, or a compromised deliverable. It is also important the project manager control who is authorized to make critical decisions for risk response because this can create further problems where individuals who are less qualified will be making important risk response decisions. This is a common occurrence on projects where little or no risk planning was performed and project staff are creating more problems in how they choose to correct problems on-the-fly on work activities.

Although reactive response mode is not preferred in most cases, lack of time and resources for proper planning often leaves the project manager in this mode where he must implement additional controls in order to operate. If authority dictates, the project manager can select individuals who are qualified to make quick response decisions and publish a list of authorized decision-making personnel to the entire project staff and management. This selected group of individuals then have the authority to respond to any risk or uncertainty and are capable of assessing the best course of action and decision for response for problems occurring throughout the project lifecycle. In this case the strategy is the use of subject matter experts to decide best responses for unplanned risks. On smaller projects, the project manager may hold the sole authority and decision-making responsibility for any and all risk responses. This would only be the case if the project manager is qualified in the subject matter and is capable of analyzing situations and executing quick responses.

Proactive Response Mode

In a best case scenario, it is incumbent on the project manager to have identified as many risks as possible and design response plans, because this puts the project manager in a proactive mode of risk response. One of the most powerful tools a project manager can have in managing projects is having information that informs him of what is planned as well as what is actually happening on work activities. The only way projects produce a deliverable that meets quality; form, fit, and function; budget; and schedule delivery is to eliminate as much uncertainty as possible so all that remains is accurate and true data, leading to a successfully project objective. The more detailed information the project manager has, the more successful he will be in this endeavor.

Planning for risks is much the same as planning for projects because the more information the project manager has regarding potential problems, the better prepared he will be in having well-thought-out response plans. This proactive approach enables the project manager time to think through responses and, in some cases, identify more than one response where the project manager can use strategy as to the best course of action. Proactive response planning also allows the project manager time to document best responses and assign ownership of particular risks to individuals who can carry out the response. This is an efficient way the project manager can oversee risk response, as preapproved responses can be assigned to individuals to be carried out in the occurrence of a risk event and do not require subject matter experts to use a cumbersome, last-minute decision process. Proactive planning in risk responses is truly the best way to manage risk for project activities; it gives the project manager much more control of not only how to respond to risk, but who can assist in risk responses being carried out correctly.

Both reactive and proactive response modes are the general condition the project manager and project staff will be in based on pre-project planning. In most cases, the assumption in risk response planning is to address problems that will have a negative effect on work activities and the project. Although in most cases this is true, occasionally an issue can result in a positive outcome that was unexpected and will also need a response. Projects, then, have the potential of both negative and positive risks.

Negative Risks

Any influence that has a negative effect on a work activity is considered to be a negative risk and results in problems that will have to be addressed. The project manager and other project staff evaluating work activities for potential risks can generally spot areas that may have a potential for a problem and will need a response plan to address the risk, should it occur. There are four typical strategies the project manager can use in addressing a risk event, which typically would take into consideration the overall risk tolerance of the project and organization as well as options that might be available for response planning and strategy project manager might use in a response that may affect other work activities within the project.

- **Avoid risk**—Identify the root cause of a risk event and eliminate or alter the conditions of the activity to create a new scenario without the potential risk. This is simply eliminating the risk before it happens and should be the best-case action in response to a risk. The caution to the project manager and project team for eliminating a risk is what actions have to be taken to eliminate or alter a condition and what effects that could have on the output deliverable for that work activity.

- **Reduce risk**—Similar to avoidance in altering the conditions of a work activity such that although it may not be possible to completely eliminate the potential risk, it can reduce the impact or probability of its occurrence. Any action that can be taken to either reduce or eliminate a risk event should be the first course of action the project manager takes in planning response.

- **Transfer risk**—Requires the reassignment of responsibility in such a way that the impact of the risk is absorbed by an alternate party. An example of this would be using an external subcontractor for a particular work activity with significant potential risk items as opposed to using the organization's internal resources, thus transferring some or all of the responsibility of identified risks out of house.

- **Accept risk**—The last course of action the project manager should use in planning a response for a potential risk event—simply accepting the outcome of the risk. There may be some conditions given a specific work activity where specifications do not allow any alteration of the conditions to eliminate, mitigate, or transfer the impact of a risk event, and the project must bear the full brunt of the impact. But this response can be acceptable as a function of risk tolerance if the specific risk event has minimal potential impact to the success of the project.

Benefits, Trade-Offs, and Pitfalls

The ability to avoid potential problems is the best course of action, given this has the least amount of impact to an original plan for an activity. This is an important factor for the project manager to consider when planning risk responses because one of the primary responsibilities of the project manager is to complete all project activities as scheduled and on budget. This being the case, the project manager would design risk responses in the best interest of maintaining the project plan and having no negative influences alter the course of that original plan. Avoidance is the only option that has maximum benefit with little or no trade-off or pitfall.

If the project manager chooses to use actions that would reduce risk or transfer risk, this usually is not accomplished without a trade-off or pitfall of some kind. The strategy for mitigating or transferring of a risk is the cost to benefit ratio and what course of action would be available that has the least amount of impact to the budget or schedule yet accomplishes the goal of minimizing the impact the risk event has. Something as simple as utilizing a claim to an organization's insurance policy to cover a particular problem transfers financial responsibility away from the project budget, leaving only residual issues with quality and delay in schedule. Contractual stipulations allow the project manager to transfer liability of a problem to another party, which opens the door for benefits, such as the subcontractor having to pay for damages, schedule delays, or quality issues.

Although acceptance might be seen as having to bear the full brunt of impact a risk event might have, it should not be seen as failure in that consideration must be made as to what level of impact the problem actually has. If a problem is unavoidable and there is no solution for transferring the risk to another party, having to accept the impact of the problem is unavoidable. It may be the only course of action. If the problem is a very large problem that may have severe impact to schedule, cost, or quality, this can be detrimental to the project. In some cases, acceptance might be the best course of action if the impact is negligible to the schedule or budget and has little or no impact on the quality of the deliverable. Designing an alternate response for a minor risk could cost the project more than simply accepting the risk impact as is. Regardless of the impact a risk has, acceptance always comes at a price because it has an influence on cost, schedule, or quality in some way, even minor, that was not originally planned.

Positive Risks

Any influence that has a positive effect on a work activity is considered to be a positive risk and an opportunity that should be addressed. Just as unplanned problems can affect work activities, unplanned opportunities in some cases present themselves where the project manager should be prepared with a response. An opportunity can manifest itself simply out of a special condition of events. In some cases, a problem or risk event, although unfortunate and still causing a problem, can also generate an opportunity that would not have been otherwise available if the problem had not occurred. Positive risks can also influence response plan designs that would give the project manager options in how to best utilize the opportunity. There are four basic response plans that can be used when an opportunity is present:

- **Exploit**—An option where the project manager would take full advantage of the opportunity, accepting all benefits that might be available. He encourages any actions to increase the probability of this opportunity to maximize the benefit that would be realized.

- **Enhance**—An option where the response is to promote further actions that would not only increase the probability of its occurrence, but more importantly increase the impact of the opportunity. The focus here is to get maximum benefit.

- **Share**—An option where an opportunity was discovered by more than one party and therefore the benefit is also to be shared by each party. An opportunity might have been discovered by one party and further enhanced by one or more parties to maximize the benefit shared by all.

- **Accept**—This is simply acknowledging that the opportunity exists and taking advantage of the opportunity if presented, but not necessarily engaging in activities that would increase its probability.

5.3 Contingency Response Strategy

If risk identification and response planning is possible at the beginning of the project, response planning will be designed around general forms of risk and only have enough detail to adequately respond to each type of risk. An example would be several work activities being performed outdoors. If weather is a problem, the response would be to delay activities or rent large outdoor tents to cover the activity zone(s), allowing work to continue. There may be cases where a much more specific risk was identified and an actual plan that specifically states actions will be carried out if certain conditions are present—this is called a *contingency response*.

By definition, a specially designed response is only carried out *contingent* on certain conditions that would warrant specific actions. A general response plan would probably be sufficient, but detailed information suggests conditions that would warrant a very specific response, and this response would be custom-designed for only one risk. Project managers can therefore design contingency responses as a form of strategy in resolving specific issues to accomplish a specific outcome.

Designing contingencies is usually seen in the case where a work activity has a specialized resource requirement (critical human resource, specialized piece of equipment, and so on), and this activity is required to take place at a specific time, where the risk will be high concerning the resource or completing the activity in the specified timeframe. With this risk being associated with this one potential problem and activity, a contingency or backup plan would have a secondary resource in place to ensure the activity is completed in the specified timeframe. The project manager may also have contingency funds set aside in the budget for this one activity to respond quickly if a secondary plan has to be implemented. How the specific contingency plans are designed can involve a strategy of how internal versus external resources are used, contingency budget planning, and schedule buffers can be evaluated for the best course of action and the least impact to the project budget and schedule.

Contractual Response Strategy

Another form of contingency planning and strategy can be seen in the use of contracts between the organization and subcontractors, vendors, and suppliers. Depending on how contracts are written, specific actions will be taken if certain conditions are met that will result in a desired outcome. These "specific actions" are contingencies designed to address a specific problem that, if it occurs, will have an automatic correction designed for the problem. Contingencies are typically written into contracts to protect one party falling victim to the other party not performing a requirement of the contract. These contingencies are known by both parties and agreed upon when the contract is signed. Contractual contingencies can include financial reimbursement, specific work to be performed at no cost, added resources to perform an activity to maintain a schedule requirement, and penalties incurred for missed schedules and poor quality.

Organizational Process Response Planning

Some organizations have project management structures such as a *Project Management Office* (PMO) that will have processes and templates that project managers can use in developing risk response strategies. Organizations that do not have formal project management structures may still have risk management processes that have been established to guide managers through the process of identifying, analyzing and developing response strategies. It is important the project manager be aware of internal processes that have already been developed as this can help expedite the work that has to be completed in developing a risk response plan. If processes exist within the organization, they can be at two levels: a *Strategic level* and the *Tactical level*.

- **Strategic level process response**—Processes developed for use at higher levels of management are more generalized, giving instruction on how to plan risk response at a higher-level overview of a project. This process might be used by a program or portfolio manager overseeing several projects or programs as a general plan they would like managers reporting to them to use in their approach to risk response. Senior management or owners of an organization may have established risk response processes to protect certain critical interests of the organization.

- **Tactical level process response**—Processes developed and used at the ground level by departmental functional managers and project managers that are specific to risks identified in work activities. This is the response plan project managers would develop that has all the detail, outlining responses to each risk, options of multiple responses, and any contingencies that have been designed for specific risks. The tactical level response, in most cases, is developed by each project manager for a specific project.

One document used typically by project managers in organizing information regarding risks on a project was discussed in Chapter 2, "Identifying Risk," which was the risk register. The risk register can be developed by the project manager to include several pieces of information regarding each risk. An example of a basic risk register is shown in Figure 5.1.

Risk Register											
Risk Priority	Description	Probability	Impact	Risk Trigger	Response Strategy	Contingency Plan	Risk Owner	Event Entry Date	Response Due Date	Actual Response Date	Manager Notes

Figure 5.1 Risk register

As shown in this example, the tactical strategy would be to include not only the response for each risk and possible contingency plans, but other information such as an assigned owner for each risk, estimated probability, and impact to the project, as well as early warning triggers that may have been identified and comments of how successful the response plan was in reducing or eliminating the risk. This type of document is valuable because it can be communicated to other project staff and management, issued to each person listed as an owner of a risk so to have all pertinent information available should a risk event occur. This document is also valuable in recording the success of risk responses for future projects.

5.4 Project Document Updates

Once the project manager has completed the process of designing response strategies for each risk, she will want to update any documents where this information would be stored. Depending on the size and complexity of projects, project managers may have only one or two documents associated with their projects or may have several that have been developed and must be maintained, which can include the following:

- Risk management plan
- Procurement management plan
- Project management plan
- Activity information checklists
- Risk register
- Master schedule (WBS)
- Master budget

Given that these documents are generally living documents in the project lifecycle, they need to be updated as new information becomes available. Some documents require authorization to include, exclude, or alter any information within the document, acting as a control document. Other documents are simply used to gather information and maintain that information for use by the project manager and other project staff and need to be updated as information changes. It's typically the responsibility of the project manager to oversee the management of these documents, what information is included and why, as well as the distribution of these documents to those needing information updates. With regard to risk, it is important updates are made quickly and accurately so that in the case of a risk event occurring, those identified to participate in the response of that risk will have the latest and most accurate information for effective risk response.

5.5 Summary

After the project manager has identified risks, analyzed the information regarding each risk, and documented risks using a tool such as the risk register that can also be used in categorizing and prioritizing risks, a response to each risk needs to be developed to reduce or eliminate the probability of occurrence and/or the impact to the project. As the project manager reviews information regarding each specific risk and the level of impact a risk may have to a work activity, it may become clear that there may be more than one option to address a potential problem.

Project managers typically like to have options with regard to managing project work activities, as this allows for variability to occur and the project manager can respond based on given variables. As a risk can have a potential impact that may result in a negative outcome to an element of a work activity, there may be different ways the problem can be addressed, depending on what the project manager is trying to accomplish. One response may cost more money but will fix the problem quickly if the project manager is buying schedule. Another response may take more time but will not cost very much money when the project manager is struggling with a project budget. The project manager can use strategy in developing responses to accomplish not only addressing a problem, but in managing the quality of the output deliverable, as well as budget and schedule.

One form of strategy is the contingency response. Contingencies may be in the form of simply padding certain costs with extra budget in case a risk in procurement occurs. Contingency may be adding extra time to a work activity task that the project manager anticipates will have a longer duration. The project manager can use contingency strategies successfully, as well as responses, as they are typically built into the project budget and scheduled before the project begins, and, if not used, simply allows more budget or schedule to be utilized elsewhere in case of a problem.

The project manager, in developing a risk response strategy process, must also record various responses and who the owner of these responses may be if not conducted by the project manager. As with other processes, the project manager needs to document all response strategies in a form that can be quickly obtained and communicated with other project staff and management.

5.6 Review Questions

1. Discuss the major components and risk response strategy using brief examples of when each would be beneficial in a particular situation.

2. Explain why the use of contingency strategies would be preferred by the project manager.

3. Explain why the project manager may not always be considered the owner of each risk and who would implement a response if the risk occurred.

4. Discuss how response strategies would best be communicated with the project staff and other management.

5.7 Key Terms

Risk response strategy

Reactive response mode

Proactive response mode

Negative risks

Positive risks

Contingency response strategy

Strategic process response

Tactical process response

5.8 PMBOK Connections (5th Ed.)

11.5 Plan Risk Responses

5.9 Case Study (Use for Chapters 5 and 6)

Corning Software Co. is a custom software development company that has been hired to develop a unique piece of software that will be used with test equipment to measure RF signals and analyze data. Specifications have been given to Corning Software to review, and a contract for development has been signed. The software package will consist of a core element of programming, data extraction, analysis and storage, and an output user interface. The software will be located on a desktop PC and will have to connect to several pieces of RF test equipment. A module will be designed that connects the PC to various pieces of test equipment.

Risks that have been identified include development of the data extraction and analysis portion of the software, successful development of an interface module that connects the PC to the test equipment, and correctly identified components on the user interface that will meet the customer's expectations.

Corning software will be using a pre-developed core module that has been tested and proven to be adequate for this requirement. Corning Software has contracted an external software designer to assist in the data extraction and analysis portion of the software. The software designer will be working with an internal software engineer, and it was discovered that the two knew each other from a previous employment and did not get along. Several attempts to contact the customer to discuss details of the user interface have resulted in a lack of information. Concerns as to the ability to develop a module that can connect the PC to test equipment have not been resolved. Modules that may be capable of this activity have been discovered and may be procured. Several pieces of test equipment will need to be purchased to perform testing.

5.10 Case Study Questions

1. As the project manager discussing information regarding risks that have been identified for this project, identify which risks may be executed in a reactive response mode versus a proactive response mode.

2. Identify negative risks as well as potential positive risks.

3. Determine if there are any contingency response strategies available.

6

Procurement Execution Strategies

6.1 Introduction

Project managers use strategies all throughout the project life-cycle from project selection, planning and execution of project activities, and even with closing and terminating the project. Strategies are also used during the execution of procurements because this process is one of the most important that is conducted throughout the project lifecycle. The project manager must work closely with those involved in the procurement of resources, materials and equipment, and facilities required for project work activities, as this directly affects all three elements of the triple constraint: cost/resources, schedule/time, and scope/quality.

As procurements are such an integral part of the project, strategy is not only used during the planning component of procurements, but in their execution as well. Many organizations have a department dedicated for purchasing, and the project manager should work closely with those individuals to assign the procurements for his project. The skills and experience of the individuals assigned to project procurements can vary greatly, and it's important both the project manager and the procurements agent understand the importance of executing the procurements in the best interest of the project and maintaining the triple constraint.

One of the most important elements of conducting business is forming relationships and the impact they can have within an organization. Most individuals responsible for procurements within an organization agree that one of the most powerful tools they have in being successful is the relationships they have established with individuals at organizations they do business with. In the interest of maintaining proper business ethics, relationship should not be established to take advantage of organizations, but to establish a connection that will be maintained for the mutual benefit of both organizations. An organization in the business of selling items appreciates the fact that they have made a connection with another organization that is pleased with their product, pricing, and delivery. Other organizations that have to procure items for their business appreciate the purchase of quality items at acceptable prices given this will be important to the success of their business. This mutual relationship is the foundation of what feeds the success of business and is driven out of mutual respect.

Another powerful tool the purchasing agent can use is historical purchases where the organization has past experience in the procurement of specific items. This can be a double-edged sword, allowing the purchasing agent to expedite certain purchases with confidence based on historical performance, but on the other hand the purchasing agent might miss an opportunity to improve pricing or some component of the purchase that would benefit the project if they do not explore other organizations for that purchase. In most cases, if an item has been purchased recently and due diligence was performed to ensure quality, price, and availability, historical purchases are usually the best option, as it not only saves time for the purchasing agent but reduces risk. Historical purchases also allow the purchasing agent the opportunity to use relationships established for these types of transactions.

This chapter focuses on many of the details in the actual execution of procurements that are important considerations that should be made in the best interest of a project with regard to cost, schedule, and quality. This chapter also shows how much work is involved in addition to planning procurements where strategy is also important in the execution of procurements.

6.2 Considerations Before Executing Procurements

When we shop for things in our private lives, it's interesting what we think about before we make our purchases and how the decision process changes as a function of the size of the purchase.

EXAMPLE

Simple purchase considerations may reflect the type of product we are considering and the purpose for its use. The purchase of a candy bar, being a consumable, would probably not be returnable once purchased. One consideration would be that I had better take extra time to decide on exactly what type of candy bar would be most pleasing for this one time nonreturnable purchase. I can't see or test the product to ensure it will meet my expectation. I may have to decide simply on historical data. On the other hand, if my wife is considering a new set of pots and pans for the kitchen, this is not necessarily a consumable, and they are displayed in the store, so she can assess which set would best meet her needs before making the purchase. She would also review the return policy to ensure that after the purchase, if the product did not meet her expectations of quality, they may be exchanged for another set or returned for a refund. These types of considerations are important, as it places value on the information required before the purchase is made to ensure the purchase will fulfill the expectations intended.

When we consider larger purchases, such as an automobile or a single family residence, many other considerations come into play: manufacturer, various options that are available, where the product is manufactured, special offers, when the product is available and any warranties or guarantees that we would expect with this type of purchase. These types of purchases are interesting given the size, complexity, and dollar amount; they are not necessarily items that can be returned for a refund; and more emphasis is placed on what type of warranties will allow any imperfections to be corrected by the manufacturer. These are examples of considerations that are made by purchasing agents when considering the purchase of various items required by project activities. Considerations are made to ensure the item purchased meets expectations and to understand options available to manage risk in the event a problem occurs with the purchase. Considerations may include:

- **Return policy**—Most purchases for project activities are either items required for the deliverable itself or items required to support the creation of the deliverable and, in most cases, would have some form of exchange or return policy associated with the purchase. The only exception is on larger projects where real estate was required to be purchased as a requirement of the project, which would have to be procured differently, in most cases through other channels in the organization than that of the purchasing department.

  One of the first and foremost considerations for the purchasing agent is the return policy offered by the organization for each purchase, as this is a primary tool used in risk response in the event a purchased item falls short of the expectations of quality and/or availability. When something can be returned in exchange for a replacement that meets quality expectations or an item can simply be returned for a refund, this allows the project team options to consider alternatives and is usually a risk response factored into each purchase. Understanding the return policy is one of the most important components of procurements the purchasing agent should know and one of most powerful tools the purchasing agent can have to ensure options to manage risk.

- **Shipping liability**—Given that most items that are purchased have to be transported to the site where they will be used for work activities, details regarding the shipping of each item have to be understood and in some cases negotiated by the purchasing agent to ensure the product still meets quality standards when delivered and at the time that was agreed upon. Details of shipping requirements are typically one of the more underestimated components of procurements, as the purchasing agents spend a great deal of time on the procurement itself, and having completed that process feel they are finished. This cannot be further from the truth, as that process only initiates the purchase and does not guarantee that the item has been successfully delivered to the project site on time and is still meeting quality expectations.

Depending on the type of product being purchased, manufacturers and distributors have packaging design to transport items to avoid damage. Manufacturers or distributors stock items in their inventory with the option of either being packaged or delivered, or the customer coming to the facility to pick the item up. This is where the purchasing agent needs to be clear as to what form of delivery was agreed upon. Some organizations have their own internal ability to manage shipping, such as having their own freight trucks, rail cars, or aircraft where they can manage the delivery of specialized materials themselves, having more control over the process of shipping to mitigate or eliminate the risk of damage. Other organizations that do not have this ability have to rely on commercial freight companies to transport items from suppliers or vendors to the project site and have to address those responsible for the shipment should something be damaged.

It is common understanding that the manufacturer or distributor that stocks a particular item is responsible for the liability of that item as long as it is in their possession. It is also common understanding that once the buyer has taken possession of an item, the liability for that item falls within the responsibility of the buyer, as the seller no longer has control of what happens to the item once the buyer has received it. The area that is not as well defined is when an item leaves the manufacturer/distributor and is in transit. Who holds the liability of the product in this transition? In most cases, the purchasing agent finds that the responsibility at this point falls onto the company contracted to deliver the part and is liable for any damage incurred during the shipping process.

This is an opportunity where the purchasing agent can make recommendations for use of a particular shipping process to ensure products are delivered to the jobsite undamaged and on schedule. In some cases, the manufacturer or distributor might have recommendations based on historical performance of a preferred shipping method that the purchasing agent might want to consider. The important aspect of shipping items that have been purchased is the purchasing agent's responsibility in not only procuring the part at an acceptable price, but to carry the procurement through to ensure proper shipping has been established to avoid damage or schedule delays.

- **Warranties and guarantees**—An important consideration for items that may have a limited return policy or no return policy at all, the procurement agent should be evaluating the purchase based on warranties or guarantees available from the manufacturer. This is typically the case on larger purchases, where the protection ensuring quality, form, fit, and function is maintained through repairs covered at no charge by the manufacturer. An example would be a large machine that was procured for a project activity where the manufacturer offers a warranty covering parts and labor for a period of time to ensure the proper function of the machine after it has been purchased and delivered. In this scenario, it would be cost prohibitive, and the schedule would not allow for the complete removal of the machine to be returned to the manufacturer for a replacement, whereas the manufacturer making repairs onsite, at their cost, resolves the issue and allows for the machine to stay in place. Warranties are a typical procurement strategy used by purchasing agents to ensure functionality of certain critical items that have to be purchased where circumstances do not allow for the return of the item in exchange for another.

- **Insurance and performance bonds**—Another procurement strategy the purchasing agents can use on critical items that are expensive or items that are custom-made is the amount of time it takes to manufacture the item and deliver to the project site undamaged. These types of items can be extremely expensive and, if damaged, can cost an enormous amount of money for repair or replacement and therefore need a different strategy to protect the project budget from excessive cost overruns. The organization can investigate the option of using an insurance policy that would cover the cost of the specialized item that the project would need. In the event of damage or catastrophic failure of a critical component, the insurance policy would cover the replacement cost of the item and can even cover any expenses in added shipping costs, project downtime, and any penalties imposed due to schedule delays. Insurance policies are primarily used to offer financial relief only and protect (reimburse) the budget.

In the case of protecting the project from external human resources contracted to perform specific work activities, a performance bond can be issued. This kind of bond protects the project from default of contract by the contractor. Performance bonds are usually issued if the buyer wants to be reimbursed for any outstanding work not performed if the contractor leaves. In some cases, the contractor, while performing work, goes into bankruptcy and does not continue. The bond would cover costs incurred by the contractor and is in place solely to protect the project budget.

- **Payment terms and options**—The next consideration made in procurements by the purchasing agent is the agreement of payment terms and conditions. This is another area that can sometimes be forgotten by the project manager and procurement agent in that once the item has been procured, delivered to the jobsite, and everything seems to be working fine, payment is another element of closing out the procurement that sometimes is left to other departments, such as accounting, to deal with. This is where the relationship between two organizations can be strained.

As we have seen, an important element in procurements is establishing relationships with those businesses from which purchases are made, and a payment plan should be part of building the trust in this relationship. The purchasing agent does not want to find he is making a phone call to ABS company thinking that he's talking to his friend only to find out the friend doesn't want to talk to him and is mad about something that happened in a prior purchase. In many cases, everything in the front part of the deal worked fine as far as the purchasing agent was concerned, but details of the payment plan slipped through the cracks, and conversations between accounting and that organization did not go well. It is incumbent on the purchasing agent to follow through with all aspects and conditions of a purchase to ensure the relationship stay strong.

Payment terms such as creating an open line of credit account allows for the purchasing agent to make purchases using an open account with the selling organization, and they can simply invoice at the end of each month for all purchases that have been made, such as a term called *net 30*. This is a procurement strategy that creates a billing relationship that can be established between the buyer's accounting department and the seller that ensures monthly invoices are paid on time. This strategy also allows the purchasing agent to make purchases that can simply be put on account and maintains a good relationship between the purchasing agent and the selling agent.

Some selling organizations do not have the capability of setting up open line accounts and prefer to be paid per purchase, so the purchasing agent should be prepared for this type of arrangement. It would be in the best interest of the project to avoid delays, such as discovering the seller of an item requires immediate payment, and the purchasing agent will need to notify accounting immediately so they can prepare payment quickly and avoid delays in shipments. Depending on the size of the organization, this can be a quick and easy process—in larger organizations, it may be more complex and require more of a paperwork trail. If the item being procured is similar in quality and can be delivered on schedule and for similar pricing, products available through another supplier that may have better payment terms may offer an opportunity to avoid risk due to payment problems.

Some suppliers and vendors that offer open line credit accounts offer a discount if a payment is made sooner than the payment term requirement; this is a strategy that allows the procurement agent to save even more money on a purchase if accounting can make a payment quickly even using an open line of credit. This type of payment strategy is called *3% 10, Net 30*. This is a regular open line of credit account with payment due in 30 days but also offers a 3% discount if paid within 10 days. Other strategies that can be used by the purchasing agent that can help ensure products are shipped on time may include the following:

- *Incentives*—Used primarily where contracts have been issued to either an individual or a company to perform work activities and an incentive is used as a motivator to ensure work is completed within a specified time frame. Incentives are used where the project schedule has critical time frames and work has to be completed on schedule to avoid resource conflicts.

  In some cases incentives are used with suppliers and vendors to award (motivate) particular actions that "if" carried out, would improve the project schedule. The project manager may approve an incentive as a low-cost way to have items delivered ahead of schedule where schedule delays may be imminent, which can be a purchase strategy that can mitigate or eliminate the risk of schedule delays.

- *Penalties*—Also used in contracting external resources as a strategy to ensure specific work is completed as specified in the contract and on schedule. It is important penalties are sized large enough that it does create a financial hardship for the contractor to make this strategy effective. There may need to be negotiation between the organization and the contractor as to the size of the penalty the contractor is willing to accept in the contract terms.

  Penalties can also be used with suppliers and vendors on critical purchases to ensure orders are filled correctly and delivered on schedule. Penalties are also used primarily in areas of the project where critical work is being performed and items that have been procured during that portion of work have to be correct and delivered on time.

- *Down payments*—In some cases are required by a supplier or vendor if a large purchase is made and a form of good faith payment on behalf of the buyer to communicate they are serious about a transaction. Down payments are most typical with work being subcontracted, as the contractor must purchase materials and requires a percentage of the overall contract price as a down payment to cover material costs. Suppliers and vendors reluctant to ship critical and expensive items may be motivated to release an item for shipment if a down payment is offered by the purchasing agent. In this case, the purchasing agent would be using a down payment as a strategy to expedite shipping to keep the project on schedule. In any case, when down payments are required, the purchasing agent should be quick to inform accounting to prepare for this kind of unexpected distribution of funds so as not to delay the procurement.

- *Fees and retainers*—Purchasing agents should be aware of all of the costs incurred in conducting procurements, some of which might include special fees that suppliers and vendors will charge in addition to the price of the item and shipping and handling charges. For example, suppliers and vendors typically charge a handling fee in addition to the price of the object and a shipping fee. Depending on the size and price of the item, handling fees can become very expensive, as these are simply an added charge to cover the cost of warehousing and packaging materials required to ship an item.

  Individuals that have been contracted for work activities sometimes charge extra fees that cover costs of work they are responsible for. An example would be hiring a subcontractor that will install electrical wiring within a home and in negotiating the contract he includes all materials and labor and permits. In this process, they might include a fee for obtaining a permit. Another example might be an individual contracted for specific work that may have fees they charge to perform certain tasks or to carry out certain activities in addition to those listed in the contract.

  Another form of fee is called a *retainer*, which is money given to professionals in in advance should their services be required. Individuals such as lawyers and specialized contractors are given retainers so they can be called at a moment's notice to perform a specialized activity. The project manager needs to be aware of these retainers if they are used with resources on their project so that these costs can be included in the overall project budget. This may not be the case if an organization has lawyers on retainer for use throughout the organization and the retainer will not be billed to a specific project, but is an operating overhead expense.

These are important for the project manager and purchasing agent to pay attention to as they can add up, given all of the work activities, items purchased, and contractors hired throughout the project lifecycle. It is important that in negotiating purchases and contracts, discussions of any hidden fees are brought up and can be identified and negotiated. The project manager will try to be as accurate as possible in estimating costs of each work activity, but unaccountable fees can incur cost overruns with the project.

6.3 Executing Purchases

When purchasing agents begin the process of actually procuring materials specific to work activity, outside of considerations that are made due to special options and strategies for purchases, certain fundamental areas of procurement are always required and should be understood by the purchasing agent. It is important all purchasing agents understand the basics of procurement to be successful in obtaining the correct items from suppliers and vendors capable of delivering quality materials and services, delivered on schedule and at the best price possible. These elements of procurement should not only be known by purchasing agents, but *understood in detail* as to the effect each of these areas have on procuring particular materials for project activities. Following are listed the basic fundamental elements of procurement and some of the important details purchasing agents should know about each element.

- **Know your purchases**—Before the purchasing agent can even make the first phone call to check price and availability on an item that needs to be purchased, the purchasing agent should know all of the details required for the item. This is a common mistake with purchasing agents, and in some cases may not always be the fault of the purchasing agent, but those supplying the purchasing agent with information for items that are required for work activities.

One would think more experienced purchasing agents would make fewer mistakes as they have more experience, but as this may be true in many cases, the devil is in the details, and any purchasing agent can overlook something and purchase incorrect items. Considering purchasing agents probably are not experienced with everything that will need to be purchased within the organization, there are some tools and techniques that purchasing agents can use to raise their awareness in times when they should ask questions as to more detail.

The easiest technique to use is in the title, description, and list of information that was given for a particular item in comparison to the same information listed in catalogs and on Internet websites.

EXAMPLE

There is a requirement to purchase a piece of pipe that that will be required on a particular construction work activity. The information given to the purchasing agent simply listed pipe: ten feet long and four-inch diameter. When the purchasing agent begins searching websites to give price and availability of this particular item, he finds out pipe is made of all kinds of different materials (both metal and plastic), has different wall thicknesses, and is rated for different materials based on what will be flowing through it. In some cases, pipes even have a temperature rating that cannot be exceeded. Some pipes come threaded on each end that will need adapters while other pipes do not have any threads and require gluing compounds or other types of adapters to connect them together. Obviously this procurement cannot proceed because the purchasing agent has discovered a lot more information that will need to be acquired to purchase the correct piece of pipe.

Although this example shows a simple purchase of a basic item, purchasing agents are bombarded with all types of products and levels of complexity that require specific information in order to obtain the correct item. The key here is for the purchasing agent to stop and ask questions about more information that is required to make the correct purchase.

- **Know your suppliers/vendors**—The second critical area in procurement is who you purchase things from. As previously mentioned in this book, suppliers are typically businesses that manufacture pieces and parts that are sold to organizations that create the final assembly of a product that will be sold. Vendors are typically distributor organizations that purchase completed items and simply redistribute them within their market, typically adding little or no value to the item, but simply assisting the manufacturer in the distribution. Two typical techniques used to assist in the evaluation of items to be purchased are

  - *Supplier/vendor list*—When organizations do business with other organizations over and over, relationships are established based on the performance of each organization. Problems typically occur through incidents such as one organization purchasing something from a seller and it being delivered later than promised, the product is not exactly what was specified and will have to be returned, or invoicing reveals that an item is priced higher than was originally discussed at the time of the purchase. These types of problems motivate purchasing agents to find another company to do business with to avoid these type of problems in the future. If the purchasing agent, in making contact with a supplier, has found an individual that was pleasant and they enjoyed talking to, understood the details of what the purchasing agent was asking for, and even asked further questions to clarify certain details, the item arrived when expected and was exactly the part that met all of the requirements, this purchasing agent will go back to this seller in the future. These are the types of relationships that help make purchasing agents successful in accomplishing their goals in supporting project procurements. The procurement department will eventually begin to list these preferred vendors or suppliers, thus creating a valuable tool for the purchasing agents in mitigating or eliminating risk and procurements due to good working relationships with supplier and vendors.

- *Historical purchases*—Another valuable technique purchasing agents can use to ensure items are purchased correctly is reviewing historical purchases. Depending on the type of projects that are carried out within an organization, in many cases certain items have been purchased time and time again, and purchasing agents can reduce their time in searching for items by reviewing historical purchases and replicating the same purchase with the same supplier or vendor. Care has to be taken at this point as to the details of exactly what has to be purchased to ensure any minor changes have been taken into consideration. The goal with this type of information is, although an item was purchased in the past, it sheds light as to the vendor/supplier, pricing, and item availability that can still be useful to the purchasing agent in expediting a purchase. It might be that only one or two small details are different and an item can be procured under virtually the same conditions.

- **You want it when?**—The next critical element of procurements is establishing when the purchased item will actually be delivered to the project site. This is another area in which mistakes are commonly made where the purchasing agent misinterprets the expected *ship date* for an expected *delivery date*. The expected ship date is when the seller is scheduled to ship the product from their facility. The expected delivery date is when the seller takes the expected ship date and includes an estimate for the time to deliver the item from the seller's facility to the buyer's delivery site. Purchasing agents must realize that in most cases the seller is estimating the time it takes to deliver an item, and this should be used with relatively low confidence. In some cases the seller can update an estimated delivery time if the shipping company can offer a tracking number for the item's shipping progress. It can be tracked, and these dates can typically be used with relatively high confidence.

  Purchasing agents should also be aware of where the item is coming from, as items purchased domestically have certain types of shipping available while items purchased from other countries have to use alternate forms of shipping, usually at a higher cost. It is also advisable that the purchasing agent, if purchasing something from another country, investigates the time it takes for items to go through customs, as this can increase the overall shipping duration and increase the risk items may not be delivered when expected.

- *Plan purchases to match project plan*—When purchasing agents are arranging shipment and delivery dates, they should consult the project manager as to the exact date items are required for work activities. In most cases, if possible, the purchasing agent should arrange to have items shipped slightly ahead of schedule to build in a buffer in case something is delayed. Unless something is difficult to store or there is a condition where an item has to be delivered on a specific day, most project managers would not mind having items show up to job sites slightly ahead of schedule to ensure work activities will continue with no downtime.

- *Expedite options*—In cases where sellers have offered an expected ship date and projected delivery date that is unacceptable for the requirement of the work activity, sellers may be able to speed up the process if they pay an expedite fee. In most cases, this simply means paying slightly extra for the seller to address their needs in front of other buyers that would have their items pulled and shipped before theirs. This can be a useful tool purchasing agents can use to avoid schedule delays, but the warning is the excessive use of expedite options with a single supplier or vendor may strain the relationship between the buyer and seller.

- *Domestic verses imported*—As we have seen, purchasing imported items can cause problems in procurements because shipments can be delayed as they go through customs to in the United States. One problem purchasing agents can run into initially is the language barrier that can present a challenge to both parties understanding each other. Depending on the type of products being purchased, purchasing agents might find it difficult to convey detailed information to sellers who speak their language; if you multiply the complexity of this problem by adding a language barrier, this increases the risk that an item will be incorrectly procured.

Another area is the value of currency between countries and problems this can cause in correctly identifying the cost of an item. With the use of the Internet, this type of problem can be eliminated as the seller can post the price of items in the currency the buyer understands. If the buyer is trying to communicate via phone message or email, this can present a challenge if the selling agent is not prepared to deal with buyers from other countries. The options in this scenario might include hiring a translator to translate email, text, or phone conversations, or to simply find another supplier. The purchasing agent should understand the importance of good communication in correctly articulating details of the items to be purchased, as this can be a potential area of risk.

- **Special conditions**—Depending on the type of products that need to be purchased, some items require special conditions that must be met in order for the procurement to be considered complete. If an item is large, expensive, or has to be custom-made, a condition might be the successful delivery of this item to the project site before the transaction is considered complete. This puts the responsibility of not only creating the item, but successfully ensuring the item is delivered to the jobsite and meets the buyer's expectations before payment will be made. Other special conditions can include product qualifications and special inspection requirements for items received from a supplier.

  - *Shipping requirements*—One of the more popular requirements or special conditions of custom manufactured items might include specific delivery and installation. The purchasing agent should recognize that although a supplier can manufacture a specialized product, that does not always mean the product will survive a delivery and be successful at meeting the buyer's expectations. Manufacturers of very large items, items that have sensitive components that can be damaged with excessive movement, or items the manufacturer has taken a long time to create will want to ensure the delivery does not damage the item purchased. These type of conditions will need to be negotiated as to who has responsibility and will pay for special shipping requirements. In some cases the manufacturer includes delivery and installation to ensure the quality of the product, whereas other manufacturers require the buyer to arrange special delivery to ensure the product is undamaged when received.

- *First article qualifications*—When an item is purchased for the first time, there can be a criteria referred to as a *first article inspection*. This refers to the buyer completely evaluating the product in form, fit, and function based on specifications that were delivered to the supplier to qualify the supplier as a valid source from which to purchase this critical item. In most cases, contractual agreements are made that stipulate after the creation of a prototype or first article, a full inspection is to be made to ensure the product was created correctly. This helps clarify between the buyer and seller that the item is being made correctly and at the quality level the buyer finds acceptable. Upon successful completion of this qualification, the purchasing agent gets approval to pursue contracts for manufacturing and scheduled shipments of the product. This type of qualification usually exists where there are critical parameters that the buyer has to be confident the seller is capable of providing.

- *Incoming inspection requirements*—A special condition where the buyer, under provisions in the contract, has requested an inspection process for all deliveries of a specific product and will be inspected based on criteria that ensures its form, fit, and function. The buyer has the right to return an item if it fails this inspection, and the seller agrees to accept the returns in exchange for items that will meet the criteria.

This condition is generally imposed as a control mechanism to eliminate risk of items requiring critical specifications to be met in order for the item to work correctly. The purchasing agent must understand why the incoming inspection would be required and on what items it will require incoming inspection. This is important in scheduling the purchase of these items to ensure there is enough time for the inspection as well as any returns and redelivery of parts so as not to create scheduling conflicts for the project work activity.

- **Pricing considerations**—Another area of consideration in executing procurements might be the opportunity to evaluate options that can improve the pricing of items that will need to be purchased. A typical mistake that is made by inexperienced purchasing agents is accepting that the seller controls the pricing and the price being offered is carved in stone and nonnegotiable. This couldn't be further from the truth; purchasing agents do have, in many cases, leverage that can be used to improve pricing or take advantage of other pricing strategies the seller might be offering that they do not always advertise. Some of the more common options that purchasing agents might investigate include volume pricing, historical pricing, and contract pricing.

  - *Volume pricing*—Although sellers might advertise a price for a particular item, they do not always advertise the fact that if multiple items are purchased there might be a reduction in price. This is called *volume pricing* and is typically established by the seller in the form of categories of pricing based on the number of units purchased. The more items that are purchased, the lower the price per item. This is beneficial for both buyer and seller, as most manufacturers' profit margins can improve given higher volume of product sold. If this is a common item that the buyer is using, and the buyer's organization has the capacity to store excess items, purchasing items in volume reduces the price of each item, making this attractive for all projects using this particular item.

  - *Historical pricing*—Another common technique used in procurements pricing is the opportunity to use pricing on items that have been purchased in the past as a negotiating tool. Depending on the relationship between buyer and seller, the type of item that is being procured, and how far in the past the item was purchased, the procurement agent can use historical pricing in cases where there might be fluctuations or variability in pricing from the seller. In cases where items offered by the seller are not purchased very often by other customers, historical pricing might be used to entice the seller to move their product as a benefit for not only the seller, but in locking in a previously agreed on price from the buyer. There may be cases where the value of an item may be in question or new pricing has been advertised by the seller, and the purchasing agent can offer historical pricing as a negotiating tool to motivate the seller to agree on a price and completed transaction. This technique is also successful when working with suppliers and vendors where the relationship is very good.

- *Contract pricing*—There are two strategies that purchasing agents can use to secure pricing during the execution of procurements:

  - **Purchasing contract**—The first type of contract the purchasing agent can use is when one organization conducts a meeting to discuss prearranged agreements on all items purchased with a specific supplier. If the buyer's organization does business often with a particular supplier, this is typically the case and the buyer would want to lock in preapproved pricing on specific items, percentage of net on certain identified items, a particular hourly wage for a service and other items that may be negotiated that lock in the pricing for purchases made between two organizations. Most purchasing agents like this kind of arrangement, as the negotiation for pricing has already been completed and the purchasing agent simply carries out the instructions of the purchase contract in procuring any items from that particular supplier.

  - **Contract agreement**—The second type of contract the purchasing agent can use is a contract agreement specific to one particular purchase that will identify specific pricing and conditions required. This type of contract in some cases is negotiated by a purchasing agent experienced with negotiating contracts or with a contract negotiator employed within the organization. This might be a contractual agreement to lease a piece of equipment for a specific timeframe, soliciting a specific service that will be performed by an organization, or the procurement of skilled individuals to perform a specific work activity. Procurement agents must understand the importance of contract agreements, as these are legal and binding arrangements between two entities, and the agent must understand the specifics of how the contract will be carried out. The procurement agent must also work closely with the project manager to make sure all conditions are met by the subcontractor before payments can be authorized.

- **Commitment correspondence**—Another important and usually underestimated component of executing purchases is communication between buyers and sellers as to what has transpired. When the purchasing agent has executed procurements, there needs to be communication between the buyer and seller as to certain critical details of the transaction to clarify for both parties what the seller will be providing and what compensation the buyer is committed to. Correspondence can be in the form of a simple receipt that can identify details of the transaction, an order acknowledgement that is sent by the seller to the buyer documenting what is intended to transpire, the signing of a bid proposal indicating the buyer agrees with the seller's proposal and wishes to commence activities, or the official signing of a contract outlining all requirements of the seller and buyer. No matter what transpires between the buyer and seller, there are certain critical pieces of information that need to be clarified and documented for both parties. Some of these critical components that need to be communicated can include

  - The names of both seller and buyer on a correspondence document.
  - Date procurement transaction was initiated.
  - Specific identification of what is being purchased.
  - Pricing or compensation of items being purchased.

- Applicable shipping or delivery arrangements and pricing.
- Some form of approval the buyer accepts the conditions of the transaction.

Because there can be a wide variety of procurement transactions for items being purchased and the type of documentation that would be associated with these purchases, the list just given is simply the bare minimum requirement that should be communicated between a buyer and seller to form a commitment to the transaction. This type of communication can be in the form of formal written proposals, a simple paper receipt that was issued by the seller, or an email form the buyer simply has to return with an approval. The purchasing agent must be aware of certain minimum details to clarify what is being purchased to help mitigate or eliminate risk in incorrect purchases due to poor communication.

6.4 Executing Contracts

The second major component in executing procurements is in managing contracts. As we have seen, contracts can be used as a strategy to manage the procurement of not only purchases, but in the acquisition of human resource labor and resources such as equipment and facilities. Depending on how the procurements department within an organization is structured, the responsibility of negotiating and executing contracts can be assigned to various individuals. In some organizations, negotiating contracts can include involvement of the accounting department, engineering, procurements, legal services, and upper management. Other organizations might leave negotiating contracts for project work activities to the project managers themselves with simple approvals by upper management. Some procurement departments have professional contract negotiators employed within the department and in combination with purchasing agents to negotiate, execute, and close contracts within the procurement department.

No matter how the organization and procurement departments are structured, the project manager must ensure that skilled and experienced individuals carry out not only negotiating contracts, but execute the conditions of the contract completely and correctly. One of the main decisions that must be made is in the use of internal resources versus the procurement of external resources, which typically results in some form of contract. The project manager, usually having this responsibility, may seek the advice of subject matter experts, functional managers, the procurement department, and upper management as to the availability of specific resources the organization might have internally to fulfill certain work activity requirements. Some of the areas of concern for making the decision between internal verses external resources is the capability to perform specific work activity requirements and availability.

- **Internal verses external resources**—One of the primary responsibilities of the project manager is evaluating each work activity as to the requirements of not only human resources, but all resources including materials, equipment, facilities, and financing that would be required to correctly carry out and complete each work activity. On larger projects, this can be a daunting task and require the assistance of project staff and subject matter experts to perform these evaluations. On smaller projects, the project manager can usually carry out this task effectively and efficiently.

  Because organizations are made up of human resources, the first place to look for completing all work activities is internal to the organization to see who would have the skills to complete each task. Depending on the size and structure of an organization, there may be some human resources that have the skill sets to effectively complete a work activity task, but inevitably due to either lack of skills or lack of availability, the project manager might have to seek external resources to complete work activities. This is an important decision, as in evaluating external resources there are things the project manager must consider for both human resources and other resources that are procured.

  - *Human resources*—The first uncomfortable area the project manager has to deal with in evaluating external human resources, is the fact that they are simply not known by anyone in the organization and no one can comment on their general personality, work ethic, and reliability. The project manager typically finds this situation is similar to interviewing someone for a job. In most cases it is probably best the project manager approach the evaluation of external human resources as a job interview, as this person will be working closely with other individuals in the organization. The project manager must know that they not only have the skills to perform the task, but they have the personality and the work ethic that will help them be successful in a project team environment.

The procurement agent may or may not have much involvement in the evaluation of human external resources but will be a part of executing the contract established between the organization and a subcontractors. Some organizations have a very controlled and organized process for the evaluation of subcontractors and how contracts are created, executed, and closed. Other organizations leave this process simply to the project manager and a purchasing agent to carry out.

It's important both the project manager and purchasing agent understand the details that have been negotiated with an external subcontractor, so there will be clarity as to certain areas of this agreement:

- Conditions under which the individual will be working on the project.
- Negotiated accommodations, if any, that have to fulfilled by the organization.
- The expectation of work performed by this individual.
- Expected delivery date of completed work.
- Details of payments to be made to the subcontractor upon successful completion of their work.

Subcontractors can be very useful on projects in that they can relieve the pressure of internal resources who may or may not be available or have the skill sets required having to perform tasks that they may not be completely capable of performing. On the other hand, subcontractors, depending on their personality and work ethic, can in some cases be a detriment to a project in not getting along with project staff, and/or creating workflow, scheduling, and other problems the project manager will have to contend with.

- *Other resources*—In addition to human resources that may be required on project activities, there is also the use of materials, equipment, facilities, and finances that may also have to be procured to complete certain work activities. Project managers sometimes find themselves enjoying the procurement of other resources over human resources, as they will not have to contend with personality conflicts and human issues that can easily cause problems on projects. Although this may be the case in many instances, other resources can also have their own issues that will result in poor quality, schedule delays, and cost overruns. These might include the following:

  - Where material is required, this is usually procured by purchasing agents as items that need to be purchased and delivered to a project jobsite. As long as the purchasing agent has all of the pertinent details to make the purchase, contracts required for material purchases will typically follow a purchase agreement format, where as long as items identified are delivered on schedule and undamaged for the price agreed upon, these contracts are fairly typical for the procurements department.

  - In many cases, contracts are used in the lease of equipment for project work activities. This can be in the form of a rental or lease agreement used to manage the acquisition of a specific piece of equipment used for a defined time period and for a specified price. These types of contracts can be simple or extremely complex, depending on the item that is leased.

    Purchasing agents, depending on their skill and experience, may choose to manage the acquisition of all equipment that will need to be leased over the project lifecycle, as they know what type of equipment is required and companies that would have this equipment available. In other cases, purchasing agents may simply manage the execution of the contract and ensure payments are made but have others locate the items required and negotiate contracts.

If the project manager uses contracts for either human resources or other resources external to the organization, it is important for him to understand the various phases of contract development and execution. During these phases, there may be specific tasks that would involve the project manager and/or the purchasing agent, and a clear understanding of each phase helps clarify any responsibilities or actions that need to be taken by either the project manager or purchasing agent. There are five primary components in using contracts that include the *pre-award phase*, *contract structure and agreement*, *award phase*, *execution phase*, and *close contract phase*.

- **Pre-award phase**—Before a contract can be written and negotiated, there must be certain evaluations made as to why the contract is needed, who the contract is with, what specific actions are to be completed, payment terms, and any special terms or conditions required by either party. During the pre-award phase, the project manager and/or project staff is making the decision to evaluate internal resources versus contracting and external resources to complete a specific work activity. This may include a make or buy decision, where the organization has the ability to manufacture a specific item required for a work activity or may choose to simply purchase this item externally. If the organization has equipment that can carry out a work activity requirement, this decision is based on the availability and the capability of this piece of equipment and the necessity of having to obtain this equipment externally. We've also seen the need for contracts to fulfill human resource requirements, whether the organization has these resources internally or needs to obtain external resources to fulfill these requirements.

These types of decisions need to be made and result in determining if a contract is required. If it is determined that an external resource is needed, there will be an evaluation as to the sources for these external resources in capability, availability, and pricing. Just because it has been determined that resources are not available internally does not always mean they will be available externally. Depending on the industry, certain pieces of equipment may not be available externally due to high demand. In the case of human resources requiring a specific skill, it may take a long period of time to identify an individual with a specific skill set willing to work under the conditions required for the work activity and for a price that is cost effective. External human resources, although identified, may not be available when needed.

The pre-award phase is also used to identify all detailed specific requirements of the external resource, which may include documentation that specifically states what the human resource must complete or what is required by a specific piece of equipment or a facility. The pre-award phase is also used for the project manager and/or project staff to identify and evaluate sources to obtain external resources and make a final decision as to what source will be selected. After the sources have been selected, structuring of a contract agreement can begin.

- **Contract structure and agreements**—The second step in developing contracts for subcontractors is to define what will be supplied by the contractor, negotiate a price, and establish a timeframe for delivery of what will be supplied, as well as any conditions that will need to be included reflecting concerns by either the contractor or the buyer. It is important that whoever is developing the contract understand what the contract is trying to accomplish, as this is usually the premise for what is included in the contract. In most cases, contracts serve the purpose of
  - Establishing a relationship between the supplier party and the buyer party
  - Documenting a deliverable
  - Establishing compensation
  - Allowing for any negotiable terms or conditions
  - Forming a legal and binding agreement

The philosophy of a contract, therefore, is a tool that two parties can use to conduct business and mitigate or eliminate risk of either party not fulfilling their side of the agreement.

- **As viewed from the subcontractor**—Contracts are used to mitigate or eliminate risk from the buyer, requiring more than what was originally negotiated for the same compensation or a reduction in compensation based on what was negotiated as a deliverable. The subcontractor uses a contract as a form of insurance policy that, if all of the conditions defining the deliverable are met within the timeframe required, compensation is guaranteed. In many cases, subcontractors are performing work before payment is actually issued, and this is in good faith, given the contract terms, that the buyer will uphold their side of the contract in providing the agreed-upon compensation in a timely manner.

- **As seen by the purchasing side of the contract (buyer)**— This also serves to ensure that the subcontractor will provide everything defined as the deliverable, with acceptable quality and within the timeframe required. The buyer is also taking a risk, from a project schedule and cost standpoint, that the subcontractor is actually capable of providing the deliverable and is not being dishonest in articulating their experience and abilities.

The construction of a contract, in many cases, may also define legal actions that will be taken if one party is not fulfilling the terms of the agreement that further establishes a risk mitigation or elimination component of the relationship. As contracts can vary greatly depending on what they are trying to accomplish, there are six basic components found in most contracts that are adequate to establishing a legal binding agreement between two parties.

- *Contract type*—The first component of constructing a contract is determining what kind of contract is needed. As we have mentioned earlier in this text, there are several types of contracts, such as fixed-price, cost reimbursement, and time and materials, that can be used based on what each party is trying to accomplish to ensure a fair and equitable business transaction, as well as the level of risk each side is willing to accept in the agreement. It is important the project manager or purchasing agent understand under what condition various contract types are used, as this will be important in not only the terms and conditions of the agreement, but in how much risk the organization will accept to accomplish the contract goal.

- *Definition of deliverable*—The second basic component in developing a contract is to define what the contractor is supposed to do; this is called the *deliverable*. One of the most important elements of the contract is for both buyer and contractor to have a clear understanding as to what the contractor is going to be doing. In many cases, risk of not delivering what was expected can be mitigated or eliminated by simply defining the deliverable at the level of detail where both parties clearly understand the intent.

  One way to check if a contract has the level of detail that the subcontractor needs to understand what is intended is when the buyer is discussing the deliverable with the contractor, how much extra explanation is required in addition to the contract to articulate what is desired. If the contract explains the deliverable well, the contractor will have few questions, and the buyer will not feel compelled to add any further explanation. If there are details that are lacking and the contractor either has to ask the buyer to clarify something or the buyer has to keep adding specific details, the contract has not been written with enough detail and needs to be modified to include a higher level of detail.

  It is also important to clarify certain specific details that are important for the buyer, as once the deliverable has been completed and something was left out, the contractor can state that he is not liable for the element that was left out, as it was not included in the contract.

  Another way to test a contract for accuracy and details is the time test. When the contractor has just finished a conversation with the person communicating the contract deliverable, it is at that point the contractor has the most accurate vision and understanding of what the buyer intends to receive. The more time that passes from that conversation to when the contractor actually begins work, the less detail the contractor remembers from that conversation and the more likely a mistake will be made if details were not included on the contract statement of work. Contractors can get very busy on several jobs, and details of any specific job can become fuzzy or can be forgotten completely. This is why the contract needs to be a standalone document—so when the contractor reads the details of what is required, it is accurate to the level of detail that will clearly articulate what was intended by the buyer, and reduce the risk of mistake or misinterpretation.

• *Negotiating price*—The third component of developing the contract can really only be completed after the contract deliverable has been defined, which is the negotiation of compensation. We use the term negotiation, as there is a value placed on the deliverable from the contractor creating it, as well as a value that deliverable has with the buyer, and this may not always be the same value.

There can be several determining factors as to how negotiating a price can be conducted and how successful each party can be at negotiating the price they feel is fair. Some of these negotiating factors may include

• Market value of the deliverable or service

• Number of special conditions or details over and above what would be considered a normal deliverable

• Level of specialized skill set required by a human resource contractor

• Availability of a specific type of subcontractor within the marketplace

• Timeframe for which the deliverable needs to be completed

• Type of contract used to structure the agreement

The project manager and purchasing manager, as well as anyone else involved in negotiating a contract, should understand that a successful agreement generally requires some level of compromise from either party to successfully reach an agreement. Sometimes this is expressing the intent of particular pricing in the contract moving back and forth between buyer and seller to narrow the pricing down to one that can be agreed on; in other cases, if one side has a particular intended price in mind, they simply compromise at the beginning and accept the price of the other side. In some cases switching from one type of contract to another can also accomplish a pricing goal by one side or the other that will be more palatable by the other side. It is generally in the best interest of an organization to have someone skilled and experienced in contract negotiation to accomplish pricing that is in the best interest of the organization and the project, and will be negotiated at an acceptable level of risk.

• *Established timeframe*—The fourth component of developing a contract is establishing a timeframe within which the contractor must complete the deliverable and the terms defining compensation. Depending on the size and complexity of the deliverable, timeframes can range anywhere from a few days to several years, and the selection of the type of contract used might have to reflect long-duration deliverables. In some cases, the contract might even call out economic adjustments over long periods of time that adjust the payment schedule to match the value of money throughout the contract.

Contractors typically solicit several buyers for potential jobs and, in some cases, may perform multiple jobs simultaneously. The project manager should work closely with the person developing the contract to ensure a deliverable that is required at a specific time is not pushed out due to contractors having other work to complete. In most cases, the timeframe for completion of a deliverable might not necessarily be a negotiable item, as the deliverable is required at a specific time in the project. In cases where a project deliverable needs to be expedited, a subcontractor will typically want extra pricing to reflect not only their cost in ensuring the deliverable is on time, but recognizes the need of the buyer and will use that opportunity to increase the pricing due to necessity.

Depending on the type of contract selected, there can be incentives for early completion as well as penalties if the contractor exceeds the allotted timeframe. This is important in the contract selection, depending on the type of deliverable and the importance of that deliverable within the project. Some deliverables, if the work activity is not on the critical path, may not be bound to a rigid timeframe and pose little or no risk, while other deliverables will have very critical delivery time specifications and pose a great deal of risk.

Care must be taken by the project manager and the contract negotiator that plenty of time is budgeted to correctly develop the contract details and negotiate with subcontractors so as not to wait until the last minute, which generally results in the subcontractor increasing prices.

- *Special terms and conditions*—The fifth component of developing a contract is any special terms or conditions by either party that will need to be included. These can include special working conditions, safety requirements, specialized equipment provided by the buyer, poor weather clause, special shipping and delivery requirements, as well as performance bonds or insurance policies taken out to cover certain aspects of the contract.

  When special conditions are included, it is best to have someone skilled in contract development and negotiation and possibly with legal experience to review how the special conditions are represented in the contract. Special terms and conditions can also include legal ramifications that can pose a risk to the organization if not negotiated correctly. Special conditions can be imposed by either side, depending on what the condition is trying to accomplish. The important element with a special condition is that both sides are aware the condition exists in the contract to avoid miscommunication or ignorance of the facts that can cause bigger problems.

- *Legal statements*—The sixth component, typically found in some inconspicuous place within the contract, is all of the legal statements defining either certain requirements of one party or the other or opt-out clauses that allow one party or the other a loophole to avoid responsibility if a certain condition isn't met. Some government institutions require certain legal stipulations to control the use of contracts, given that in most cases contracts are legal binding documents.

- **Award phase**—The award phase typically follows deliverable definition and contract development because this is when contracts are actually discussed with potential contractors. The first element of this phase is selecting the contractor, and this is done generally by soliciting several contractors to view a particular statement of work and potential contract conditions to see who would be interested. This can be accomplished through contractors submitting proposals or bids in response to a statement of work where the buyer can evaluate the response of each subcontractor.

When reviewing proposals and bids from subcontractors, care must be taken to understand their interpretation of what the statement of work is calling out. This might be the first sign of trouble as to whether a contractor is experienced with this type of work and knows the details involved versus lesser experienced contractors who may not pick up on certain critical details. The buyer can also evaluate proposed pricing to see which contractors have realistic figures. It is advisable the buyer have a detailed conversation with each proposed contractor to ascertain the level of professionalism, the type of company they represent, and how they conduct themselves and answer detailed questions concerning various aspects of the deliverable. In some cases, contractors are dismissed from the process based on the outcome of a simple conversation.

The process of review and selection of a subcontractor might require several conversations to gain more information to complete the decision. In some cases a subcontractor might have been selected based on discussion of the deliverable, but the relationship was strained when contract negotiations of time frame, pricing, and possibly special conditions were not agreeable. This is when an experienced contract negotiator can successfully discuss the terms of the contract and make appropriate compromise, driving to a successful agreement.

Once the contractor has been selected and a successful negotiation of the contract terms and conditions has been completed, both parties must document acceptance of the contract, typically in the form of a signature or stamp of approval that officially awards the contract to the subcontractor and affirms the legal binding agreement.

- **Execution phase**—Once the contract has been signed by both the subcontractor and the buyer, commencement of the contract terms and conditions can begin, and the subcontractor can proceed with their responsibility concerning the contract deliverable; this is called the *execution phase*. During the execution phase, all work required by the subcontractor is performed, including any special conditions by either the subcontractor or the buyer, and needs to be met to ensure the project deliverable is successfully completed.

  There may be conditions in the contract that require scheduled payments throughout the execution phase, as requested by the contractor. Depending on how long the contract duration is, this may be cash required by the contractor for the purchase of materials and equipment and to cover operational costs such as salaries and business expenses during the course of completing the project deliverable. If the contractor is a special skilled resource, this may simply be salary compensation, defined as regular payments throughout the contract period.

  The project manager is most active during the execution phase in monitoring the progress of work by the subcontractor to ensure compliance to the contract and that the contractor's quality is meeting expectations. It is also important the project manager monitor the subcontractor's progress to ensure it stays within the project activity timeframe requirements.

- **Close contract phase**—Once the project deliverable has been successfully completed, and all terms and conditions have been met within a given contract, the contract can then be closed. This is a very important phase in the duration of a contract where the contractor determines they have completed the deliverable per the conditions of the contract and feel they are finished. It is important the project manager and purchasing agent, if applicable, evaluate the completion of a contract deliverable to ensure it meets the quality, form, fit, and function outlined in the contract statement of work. It might be advisable to solicit subject matter experts to evaluate the completed deliverable to ensure it has met the intended expectation of what was desired for the work activity.

- **Buyer concerns**—Although the closing phase might appear to be fairly easy, it can actually be one of the most complex and stressful times during contract duration. Because contracts can range from very simple to enormously complex, care must be taken by the buyer to ensure the deliverable meets the expectations called out in the contract. This might include inspection of any specific details, any change requests that have had to be included, and any other specifics that could likely have been forgotten by the contractor. In some cases, if contractors are short on time or resources and have to hurry to complete a deliverable, shortcuts might be taken, such as using inferior materials, a reduction in quality of workmanship, or simply forgetting something altogether. It is incumbent on the project manager to ensure everything that was negotiated in the contract has been delivered and meets the expectations of the buyer.

- **Contractor concerns**—The closing phase is equally important to the subcontractor, as it is at this point the subcontractor receives final payment for completing the contract deliverable. Subcontractors generally feel the highest risk of a problem is in getting final payment, as the buyer will ultimately try to find some nonconformity that will allow a reduction in payment. Subcontractors may also have had special conditions written into the contract that they will need to make sure were fulfilled by the buyer.

Closing a contract can be stressful for both buyer and subcontractor, as this finalizes the agreement and both parties have to determine if the other party has fulfilled their parts of that agreement. This is typically a time of highest risk for both parties, as well as of problems that may not be easily resolved. In some cases, a moderator might have to be hired to facilitate further discussion concerning the closing of a contract and certain contract terms and conditions that may be impeding the closing process.

Once the buyer and subcontractor are in agreement that the terms and conditions of the contract have been fulfilled, the buyer can release final payment to the subcontractor, and the contract is considered closed. It is important to note that in some cases subcontractors (generally feeling they were not paid enough for the deliverable) return with accusations that the buyer still has some piece of equipment or something was stolen at the project site, and they want the buyer to replace it or require the buyer to compensate the subcontractor in some way. Be careful with these type of contractors—in some cases these stories might be true, but they are generally manufactured to collect more money from the buyer.

6.5 Results of Executing Procurements

Once contracts have been successfully completed and closed, it is important that project-related documentation is updated with the conclusions and results of completed contracts. This needs to include the results of successful contracts, as well as contracts having issues that needed to be resolved and contracts that had to be terminated prematurely. This is especially important to use as a communication tool as well as officially documenting what transpired in the course of the contract. Information relating to contract activities might be important for the following reasons:

- Capturing details of contract activities as they are fresh in everyone's mind.
- Details of contract negotiation techniques, successive contracts chosen, and any contract strategies can be documented and communicated to contract negotiators and the procurement department.

- The procurement department might also be interested in the success of particular subcontractors, as this can be valuable information in selecting subcontractors to perform similar duties in the future.

- This information is also valuable in lessons learned documents so other project managers can learn from the mistakes and successes of contracts and subcontractors used on prior project work activities.

As the project manager conducts work activities throughout the project lifecycle, she will be interested in updating project documents to communicate progress of work activities in the overall project objective. This can include updates that may be made to the work breakdown structure and master schedule, budgetary updates and assessments to baseline estimates, information relating to risk responses and contingencies, as well as notations to project information checklists for future use. Some of the primary documents the project manager will most likely update are

- Project management plan
- Cost management plan
- Schedule management plan
- Quality management plan
- Risk management plan

6.6 Summary

One of the most stressful times during each project work activity is executing the actions that have been planned for months that involve the planned purchases and contracts to actually be initiated. This is when the project manager and individuals in the procurement department need to be on high alert to make sure purchases are conducted correctly and contracts are initiated on time.

The purchasing agent's job is to buy things, so you would think this would be a normal activity that is carried out on a daily basis, but in some cases special procurements for project requirements are stressful because of schedule and budget requirements. It is important the purchasing agent know his suppliers and vendors well and have a full understanding of all the details of what needs to be purchased to ensure the transaction starts off on the right foot. As all items that need to be purchased have been estimated in the project budget, it is also vitally important the procurement agent secure pricing that is at or below the original estimated costs to ensure procurement will stay on budget. The purchasing agent also needs to confirm delivery schedule and method to ensure critical items are at the work activity site on schedule and undamaged. The project manager must work with the purchasing agent to ensure payment is made, which may include communicating with the accounting department of the organization.

It is also vitally important contracts are initiated on time and correctly as to not incur disputes or problems that would delay work being performed by a subcontractor. Contracts can also be used in leasing equipment or facilities required by the project. These agreements need to be negotiated in advance so that when they commence, the project stays on schedule and on budget.

The project manager needs to be aware that conducting procurements does pose a risk to the project, and care should be taken to oversee procurement activities to ensure problems do not occur. Many things happen in the course of a project work activity, and conducting procurements can play a role in ensuring all aspects of work activity run smoothly or can introduce problems affecting the quality of the output deliverable for the work activity as well as the budget and schedule.

6.7 Review Questions

1. Discuss why conducting procurements during a project work activity can be stressful for the project manager.
2. Lists some of the key areas in executing purchases and why some of these areas pose a risk to the project.

3. List the key components in the pre-award phase of executing a contract and discuss how the project manager would need to be involved in the pre-award phase.

4. Discuss the importance of preferred supplier/vendor lists.

6.8 Key Terms

Conduct procurements

Executing purchases

Executing contracts

Commitment correspondence

Pre-award phase

Award phase

Executing phase

Close contract phase

6.9 PMBOK Connections (5th Ed.)

12.2 Conduct Procurements

6.10 Case Study Questions (Use Case Study in Chapter 5)

1. Discuss purchases that would be executed.

2. Discuss executing contracts and what terms and conditions may be included that could manage risk.

3. Outline the pre-award, award, and execution phases of a contract used in this case study.

Part III
Integrated Monitoring and Control

After the project manager has officially started the project and work activities are underway, it is assumed a risk management plan and a procurement management plan are in place. One important element included in each plan is the development of a monitoring and control system. As the project manager has invested time developing the risk management plan, which includes identification of risks, analysis of risks, and the development of risk response strategies, it would render their work pointless if work activities were not monitored for imminent risks. The critical element in being proactive, with regard to risk, is not only having identified the potential risks, but also watching for signs of this risk occurring and being ready with the response strategy. Developing a monitoring and control system enables the project manager to not only be aware of a potential risk, but to possibly see early signs of a developing problem, allowing for more time before a risk occurs to reduce or eliminate it.

This is also the case in conducting procurement. Even if quality planning goes into a procurement strategy, it does not do much good if procurements are not being monitored and controlled. The project manager can collaborate with purchasing agents and individuals in the accounting department of an organization to brainstorm various ways to monitor and control items being purchased and contracts being negotiated. It is important for the project manager to ensure purchases and contracts are being conducted correctly and with minimal risk. Managing procurements is actually included as a potential risk throughout the project lifecycle, and the project manager should be aware that problems are likely to happen when items are being purchased and contracts are initiated and executed.

The project manager must understand the importance of developing good monitoring and control tools, as this is how the project manager and staff will truly be proactive in managing both risk and procurement throughout the project lifecycle. In many cases, monitoring and control tools and techniques are surprisingly simple to develop and use, and they yield powerful information the project manager will need in controlling risk and procurement; how this information is used can mean the success or failure of a project.

7

Risk Monitoring and Control

7.1 Introduction

Organizations are faced with the reality of risk on a daily basis, and how the organization plans for problems and responds to those problems can be largely responsible for whether an organization is successful or struggles. Projects are similar as problems and risks due to uncertainty will always be a component of projects, and project managers have to plan for the worst to ensure the highest probability of success for their projects. This book covers five primary components of managing risk on projects which include:

- Identifying potential risks
- Analyzing risk information
- Planning risk responses and contingencies
- Monitoring and controlling risk
- Closing risk events

We have already studied identification, analysis, and planning risk responses, so it is time to explore how the project manager and project staff monitor and control risk. One of the most important elements of dealing with potential risks is to understand the difference between reacting to a problem after it has happened and being proactive in planning for problems before they occur. As we have covered previously, we know reactive responses typically do not offer many options and generally result in budget overruns and schedule delays. We also know that proactive planning for potential problems allows for more evaluation of options where the project manager and project staff can actually plan responses for various types of issues or eliminate a risk altogether. This is effective in not only preparing for risk, but helps to reduce to cost overrun and schedule delays.

The last element in proactive risk planning would be to develop monitoring tools that can be put into place throughout the project that would give indications if previously identified risks might be imminent and controls can be initiated to help mitigate or eliminate potential risk. This chapter explores tools and techniques that can be put in place to do just that. Establishing a risk monitoring and control system integrates risk planning directly into the project plan and gives the project manager and project staff the tools they need to proactively address potential problems in real-time. The project manager usually feels more confident about managing project work activities when an integrated risk monitoring and control system has been developed and put in place, truly placing him in the driver's seat to control all aspects of the project.

7.2 Risk Monitoring Techniques

If the project manager is skilled and experienced with developing a project management plan, he will be aware of what monitoring activities actually mean, given that this is typically performed in monitoring quality of work activity performance, costs, and schedules. The project manager knows that monitoring aspects of the project is important because this gives him real-time data as to how the project is progressing. This also indicates areas where the project manager might have to make adjustments, which are typically called controls, that are designed to bring the nonconforming element of the project back into acceptable limits. These forms of adjustments can only be accomplished if someone is actually paying attention to what is going on via an integrated monitoring system.

For project managers who are not skilled or educated in formal project management plan structure, the aforementioned areas of concern, quality, cost, and project schedule, make up what is called the *triple constraint*. These are called constraints due to the fact if a problem occurs affecting one of these three areas, it will likely affect one or both of the other areas. In a formal project management plan, the project manager not only has to initially develop a work breakdown structure of how the project deliverable will be broken down into smallest components, but estimate all costs and schedule duration requirements of each work activity. To ensure that during the execution of work throughout the project lifecycle, quality is being maintained as well as the cost of all items procured and work is staying on schedule, the project manager will have to monitor these aspects of the project. This requires the development of an integrated monitoring system.

The development of an integrated monitoring system starts with determining what risks have been identified and how areas of project work activity can be monitored to determine when a problem is imminent. The first part in developing the integrated monitoring system is to look at information sources that would suggest where risks might occur and where monitoring needs to be developed.

- **Information sources for risk monitoring**—When the project manager is developing an integrated risk monitoring system, she must first understand what risks there will be, as this will be important in what type of monitoring should be established. The project manager, in developing the risk management plan, has probably completed the risk identification and response components of that plan; the first place for gathering information on potential project risks would be the documents created in the risk management plan.

  - *Activity information checklist*—One of the most important documents that that can be created for each work activity, it lists all the specific details required in each activity. This typically includes any potential risks and comments from subject matter experts and those experienced with that activity as to what responses would be successful and any early warning signs that would indicate a problem would be imminent. The project manager typically uses the activity information checklist as the foundation for all detailed information on which to build the rest of the project management plan because this document is at the ground level of detail that would most likely reveal potential risks.

- *Risk register*—In developing the risk management plan, another important document the project manager creates is called the *risk register*, which organizes all information regarding each risk. The risk register can be developed to include all kinds of information regarding each risk including:

  1. Categorization and prioritization of all risks

  2. Probability and impact of each risk

  3. Responses and contingencies

  4. Owner identified for each risk

  The risk register can also include the monitoring tools that have been developed for each risk and what information the project manager would expect to see from each monitoring tool.

- *Risk management plan*—When the project manager begins a new project, there are several areas within the project management plan that the project manager must address and develop to understand more of the details of what has to happen to successfully complete a project objective. One of the items included in the overall project management plan is a Risk Management Plan. The risk management plan is basically a template document that the project manager uses on all projects to ensure that everything required in planning for risk has been accounted for and completed.

  Areas in the risk management plan include:

  - Identification of risks

  - Risk analysis

  - Risk response planning

  - Controls developed to manage risks

  Developing the integrated monitoring and control system would be included in the risk management plan under the control risk section and would include all information regarding tools, techniques, and any other pertinent information documenting how the project manager has developed the monitoring and control system.

- *What risks are we watching for?*—In developing the integrated monitoring and control system, the project manager, after evaluating the information of potential risks throughout the project, must decide what risks should be monitored and controlled.

  Depending on the size and complexity of a project, there could be a short list of potential serious risks or an exhaustive list outlining hundreds of risks that will need to be monitored. In most cases, examining the risk register reveals that risks have been prioritized generally in three categories:

  - Impact on quality of work activity
  - Project schedule
  - Project budget

  Inside of these primary categories the project manager prioritizes risks due to impact and severity using three categories:

  - Severe
  - Moderate
  - Mild

  Upon evaluation of the risks in each category and the prioritization of each category, it is advisable to design monitoring for the severe and moderate categories. As risks prioritized in the mild category have little or no impact and little or no probability of occurrence, it is advisable to look at the responses that were developed and, in many cases, will probably find that the risk is simply inconsequential and therefore simply acceptable if it occurs and does not require monitoring. Monitoring needs to be established for the severe and moderate categories, as these are more likely to occur, have more impact on the project, and may shift in prioritization throughout the project lifecycle, where moderate risks can move into the severe category and vice versa.

- **Develop early sign triggers**—In developing documentation for the risk management plan, the project manager and other project staff have identified potential risks, assessed the relative probability of occurrence and impact the risk could have on the project, as well as developed a response plan for each risk. One of the primary components in developing an integrated monitoring system is to evaluate each risk and determine if there are any early warning signs that can be identified that would suggest a problem is about to occur.

To assist in this task, the project manager should solicit the help of subject matter experts and anyone else within the organization that would have experience with a particular type of risk to discuss what early warning signs might be available for each risk. Early warning signs, sometimes referred to as *triggers*, are typically found in the events leading up to a potential risk. The project manager, knowing all of the work being performed within each work activity, cost, and schedule requirements of each work activity would see this as normally scheduled and operating as expected to the project baseline of cost and schedule. In the course of a work activity, if events are unfolding that are yielding unexpected information, this would be an early warning sign that a problem might be imminent.

Early warning sign triggers are important in developing monitoring tools, as the function of monitoring would expect to see a work activity under normal operation and would be looking for any early warning signs to indicate a problem might be imminent. This is why triggers are used: they are visible while monitoring work activities, indicating non-normal activity. Triggers can be developed based on several different aspects of a work activity that may indicate either the development of a problem or that a problem is about to begin. In developing early warning signs, the project manager would go back to the risk register and categorize early warning signs based on quality of work performed, schedule, and budget. Examples of early warning signs within each of these three categories can include the following:

- *Quality of work performed*
    1. *Observations of poor quality at the beginning* of the work activity that can be corrected early. The risk or outcome of poor quality being realized at the end of the work activity often results in failure and rework.

2 Evaluations of *go/no go* or *pass/fail inspections* of smaller components of work as the activity progresses.

3 *Workers commenting* on work being performed and/ or obvious lack of experience or skill of a coworker that might put the outcome of the work activity at risk of poor quality or being incomplete.

- *Work activity schedule*

  1. *Observations of slow progress at the beginning* of a work activity that, if continued, will result in finishing behind schedule.

  2. *Discussions before a work activity begins* that would suggest that a critical resource may not start as scheduled or may not be available at all.

  3. Rumors of *change orders that may add additional work* on one activity may cause other work activities to fall behind schedule.

  4. *Early news reports that predict adverse weather* conditions, which may pose a delay in work activities.

- *Work activity budget*

  1. *Early discussions with the procurement* department concerning developments with future purchases, indicating potential price increases.

  2. *Signs of schedule delays* that may require an increased number of resources, at additional cost, to complete an activity on schedule.

  3. *Early news reports that predict adverse weather* conditions that would result in unacceptable delays in work activities that require tents and covers at additional cost to protect the jobsite to avoid delays.

- **Monitoring tools**—The process of establishing an integrated risk monitoring system involves the development of information gathering tools designed to monitor work activities that will provide early warning indicators to alert the project manager and staff of a potential risk. These tools can be categorized at two levels within the project:

- *Project level*—Information at the project level typically comes in the form of status updates, workflow analysis, and procurements reports. Monitoring tools to gather information at the project level might include
  - Status meetings
  - Project status correspondence (email, reports)
  - Casual discussions with project staff
  - Resource allocation meetings with functional managers
  - Subject matter expert interviews
- *Activity level*—Information at the activity level is typically much more detailed, and monitoring systems are in place to gather specific information about actual tasks within the work activity. Monitoring tools to gather information at the activity level might include
  - Task completion check charts
  - Work inspections
  - Regular reviews of scheduled procurements
  - Weekly weather reports
  - Daily or weekly observations of specific work activity

Monitoring tools designed to gather information are useful for the project manager and any project staff assigned to evaluate the potential for risks. It should be noted that using information gathering techniques should be designed to not only identify risk events that may occur, but more importantly indicate early warning signs that could allow the project manager extra time to take action before risk materializes.

7.3 Risk Control Techniques

Monitoring is the process of gathering information that would reveal indicators that a risk is imminent; controlling risks are the actions taken based on the analysis of the information gathered, as to corrections that will be implemented to adjust the conditions of a work activity to mitigate or eliminate a potential risk. The characteristics of control are different than monitoring in that control is an action taken to change a condition that will influence the outcome of a work activity, whereas monitoring is information gathering looking for early warning signs or triggers of a potential risk. In this section we will look at five areas within project management where control tools can be designed and implemented to manage risk.

- **Quality control**—Quality control generally is in reference to the creation of a project deliverable or the outcome of a service rendered. Projects typically have a documented deliverable that requires the completion of each work activity. This documentation also includes materials that will be used, the amount of time it should take to produce a deliverable, and the expected characteristics and functionality designed in the requirements of that work activity deliverable. The measurement of how a deliverable is produced can be defined as its *quality*. Quality is meeting the expectation of the customer for a product deliverable or service and is typically defined in two general terms:

  - *Intended functionality*—Refers to the production of a deliverable that accomplishes all of the originally designed characteristics and functions required by the customer. When a deliverable is evaluated against the original specifications, drawings, or documented intentions of functionality, the quality standard is that it meets or exceeds the expectations of the customer receiving the deliverable.

  - *Materials and workmanship standards*—Refers to the types of materials and the level of expertise of human resources, machines, or equipment used in producing the deliverable. This criterion is different from functionality because a deliverable can meet all of the functionality expectations but be created out of *materials* that do not meet the customer's expectations. This can also be referred to as a deliverable meeting all of the functionality and created with materials that meet the customer expectations, but created by human or equipment resources that yields workmanship that does not produce an end product that meets the customer expectations. Because this can be a rather subjective assessment, this measure of quality has to be defined in the activity requirements regarding specific materials in the form of workmanship standard that would be acceptable by the customer.

Tools that can be used to control quality would need to be designed to perform both an inspection and a stop work activity function to discontinue the creation of any further nonconforming work.

- *Quality inspections*—Projects that have work activities that produce tangible items can incorporate tools that can inspect these items all throughout their creation. At any point in the creation of an item, if an inspection reveals nonconforming work, progress is halted, and the changes are implemented that will correct the process creating the nonconformity. When the creation of the item continues and the inspection process reveals the nonconformity no longer exists, the control mechanism was successful in ensuring the outcome of the work will meet quality standards.

  And in projects where the output deliverable is a service that is performed, quality inspections can include a second party to observe the service being performed. If the inspection reveals that a particular aspect of the service is being performed incorrectly, the service can be stopped, adjustments can be made, and the service can resume, resulting in acceptable performance.

  In both of these instances, quality inspections evaluate information, perform a stopgap initiative that allows for a correction that influences a condition such that a corrected nonconformity sidesteps a potential risk of failure at the completion of the work activity deliverable.

- *Regulatory inspections*—Similar to quality inspections, these inspections are initialized through requirements of a local, state, or federal government agency in conjunction with a permit that was issued or requirements based on specific characteristics of that deliverable. An example of a regulatory inspection would be in the construction of a building where a building permit was issued by a local government agency. An agency representative makes regularly scheduled inspections to ensure construction conforms to regulatory requirements of the building permit. This helps ensure construction of the building meets the local code requirements and will be built correctly.

- *Design reviews*—Used within an organization that utilizes engineering resources or development type resources as stop points during the production of items like a prototype. These types of product deliverables are broken up into major phases and have milestones or stop points where engineering, subject matter experts, and management staff can evaluate the progress of work activity. Design reviews serve as a form of control in which information on the work activity performance is gathered and analyzed, but work activity is halted upon review of this analysis to determine whether alterations have to be made or whether work can proceed as planned. This type of control also includes a stopgap measure to ensure quality before progress is allowed to continue, avoiding failure at the completion of the deliverable.

- **Schedule control**—The second element of project control the project manager needs to consider is controlling the amount of time spent conducting a work activity. Depending on the size and complexity of a project, this task can be very simple, or it can be incredibly difficult given an extremely complex work activity. The project manager must remember that control is required only if the information gathered on a work activity has been analyzed and suggests that a parameter of activity duration has shifted beyond acceptable limits.

As control generally results in action required to adjust conditions that will bring work activity progress back on schedule, it is recommended the project manager establish a change control process, as schedule control typically involves change of some kind. Depending on the type of work activity, there may be several options as to how the project manager can control activity duration, but in some cases may have limited options and change may be inevitable.

The most important component of schedule control is the data gathered that would suggest work activity is falling behind schedule. It is recommended that the project manager use only the data gathered directly from work activity to use for analysis, as the basis of considering any type of change in work activity to correct an activity duration problem. It is important the project manager use first-hand information to determine if activity duration has become a problem because any further corrections or change that might be implemented will be based on this information. It is common to derive schedule information formally through casual conversation, but this information may simply be someone's opinion or subjective observation and not valid. The warning for the project manager is before actions are taken; verify any information as being valid.

Tools that can be used to control schedule should be in the interest of avoiding potential risk and falling behind schedule, therefore creating other problems such as schedule conflicts with available resources, critical work activities scheduled for a specific time that may be at risk, and cost overruns due to schedule related problems. Following are some of the more commonly used schedule control tools that are successful in managing risk:

- *Critical chain method*—The critical chain method (CCM) is a control tool that implements buffers within project activities at specific locations to control the project schedule. The critical chain utilizes the critical path approach of network diagramming project activities and is most effective in resource utilization and optimization. Buffers are represented similarly to activity items connected within a path that are identified as non-work activities but have duration. The primary philosophy in the use of buffers is to balance pathways to accomplish corrections in schedules to avoid the risk of single activities that have fallen behind schedule converging with other activities, putting the whole project at risk of being behind schedule. Buffers can be utilized in two primary areas within the network of activities:

  - *Feeding buffers*—These buffers are placed on specific paths that need influence to control the cumulative schedule durations for a particular path.

- *Project buffers*—These buffers are placed on the main or critical path to control the overall duration of the project schedule.

Examples of the use of both feeding buffers and project buffers are shown in Figure 7.1. Here, the convergence of two paths of project activities into the critical path of project activities might have to be adjusted using buffers. A buffer might be placed in the main critical path toward the end of the chain of activities to help protect the finish date and stay in compliance with the baseline of duration estimates and the expected project completion date.

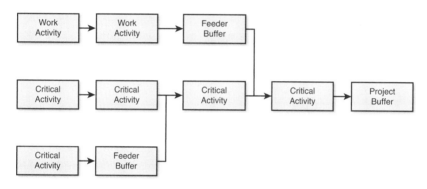

Figure 7.1 Critical chain method

- *Schedule crashing*—If the project manager is faced with a critical time constraint for a particular work activity, she must look at the triple constraint to see how the elements of cost/resources and scope/quality would be affected. The project manager would typically not have the ability to reduce quality in order to complete the activity on schedule, so she would look to the availability of more resources to complete work activities on time. Schedule crashing is a technique the project manager can use that simply increases the use of a particular resource on a work activity to mitigate or eliminate the risk of going over schedule on that activity. Adding resources to a work activity typically requires added cost to the project budget.

The key feature of this technique is selecting the least costly resource that can provide the greatest amount of reduction in schedule duration. This method is especially effective as a control technique because activity duration can be greatly reduced if financial resources are available to add resources to complete work activity on schedule to eliminate that potential risk. Crashing should be used only in controlling the project schedule if no other options are available because it usually adds to the budget.

- *Fast tracking*—If it is determined that the duration of a sequence of activities is too long and needs to be reduced to maintain the schedule, another form of schedule reduction within a particular path of work activities is called *fast tracking*. This technique is used to compress the overall duration of a group of work activities by shifting work activities from being in serial (one after the other), shown in Figure 7.2, to performing work activities in parallel (consecutively). The project manager needs to review the predecessor/successor relationships and dependencies of neighboring work activities to determine whether performing two activities in parallel would be an option. This is an excellent way to reduce the schedule of a particular path of activities at no added cost to the budget. An example of fast tracking is shown in Figure 7.3.

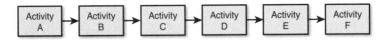

Figure 7.2 Standard serial network of activities

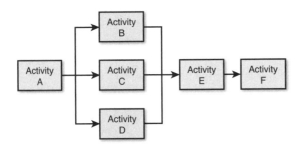

Figure 7.3 Fast tracking work activities

• **Cost control**—Depending on the size and complexity of a project, controlling cost will have the project manager evaluating costs that may be objective and well-documented, and costs that although started as estimates might be more subjective and seem elusive to try and understand, let alone control. The project manager, in developing the budget at the beginning of a project, must try to establish as many actual costs as possible and reduce the number of estimates to reduce risk in the procurement process. This can be accomplished through the use of certain types of contracts and the use of proposals and bids where suppliers or vendors have expressed fixed prices and the purchase or lease of items have a published price. The project manager's difficulty in controlling the cost of a project typically is found not so much in the procurements, but in added cost in the course of the project lifecycle, maintaining quality and activity durations to stay on schedule. In most cases, controlling cost can be narrowed down to three approaches:

  • *Cost control through a refined budget estimating process*— One of the fastest, most accurate, and least expensive ways to control cost that would have the least effect on the other two components of the triple constraint is to have accurate cost estimates at the beginning of the project. Most project managers agree that there's nothing more frustrating than to have a budget full of estimates that have questionable reliability. When the project manager is trying to manage work activities, procurements and schedules, the last thing he needs is to be told is that the original pricing is not accurate and that the procurement department is reporting higher prices.

  The first order of cost control on a project has to do with the project manager himself and the time spent creating an accurate budget. When proper time is spent at the beginning of the project, the project manager can develop a budget based on fixed price commitments from contractors, suppliers, and vendors that will be agreed upon by both parties and be counted is accurate. This type of control is built-in at the beginning and can mitigate or eliminate procurement cost overruns.

- *Cost control through organizational procurement processes*—The second area of cost control is in controlling the procurements process. As just mentioned, the best gift the project manager can give the procurement department is a project budget based on committed and published costs that simply needs to be executed when required. These types of budgets have much lower risks because committed and published prices are less likely to change. The problems in the procurement process where risks are greater fall into two general areas:

  - **Budgets using estimates**—When the project manager is unable to obtain commitments on firm pricing for certain budgeted items, he is left with the process of estimating, which is simply a best guess based on whatever information he could obtain. What this really says is the project manager has to put in a placeholder amount in the budget, and procurement must identify the actual cost when the item is required in a work activity.

    Unfortunately, the inaccuracy of estimating increases the risk of cost being higher at the time items have to be procured. The best control at this point, if an estimate is all the project manager can produce, is to try and seek out as much information possible to improve the accuracy of the estimate. Another form of control is to add a buffer or additional amount on top of the estimate as padding to ensure at the time of procurement the actual cost is either equal or less than the estimate plus additional buffer.

  - **Organizational procurement processes**—Another area of concern is the processes used by the procurement department and the personnel who carry out procurements. Organizations typically have procurement or purchasing departments, and the processes used can either introduce control or require control. One example is the use of preferred vendor/supplier lists, where sellers have been evaluated for their performance and the best suppliers and vendors have been identified to conduct business. This is an excellent control process used by the procurement department, as the relationships between the organization and businesses on this list help to reduce risk in pricing, quality of products, and commitments to delivery.

Another example would be whether the procurements department has an experienced contract negotiator, or if the purchasing agents simply attempt to negotiate contracts on their own. Experienced contract negotiators understand the strategies of different types of contracts and what elements within the contracts present more or less risk.

Another form of control by the procurement department is purchase verification, where the purchasing agents verify the costs on particular items to ensure the purchase is made correctly and at a cost the project manager is aware of. These types of controls used by the organization in the procurement department are important in helping to control project costs.

- *Cost control through managing project quality and schedule*—The project manager usually finds controlling costs most difficult in maintaining the quality of work through each work activity and ensuring work activities are completed on schedule. So the project manager, in controlling costs, actually focuses on controlling quality and schedule, and this is why these three components (cost, schedule, and quality) make up the triple constraint. If the project manager has developed an accurate budget of as much fixed or published pricing as possible, procurements will be secondary to controlling cost overruns in managing work activities. In many cases, the project manager finds more risk and higher cost overruns managing the scope and quality of project deliverables and trying to keep project activity on schedule.

- **Scope control**—The next area of control has to do with the products or services that are produced to accomplish the project objective. In as much as the customer tries to articulate expectations of what they wish to obtain through the project endeavor, in many cases, that seems to only be the starting point; changes occur throughout the project lifecycle that refine what the customer needs. When the project manager is developing the overall project management plan that will include the definition of any deliverables or services, she is actually defining two things—the scope of the project and the scope of the deliverable or product.

- *Project scope*—At the beginning of a project, a customer defines a deliverable or service in great detail, but once this process is completed, the project manager then begins to build a project plan that includes all of the activities to not only create the deliverable, but project activities that will be needed to support work activities; this is called the *project scope*. When the project manager is looking to control how much work is actually going to be required to accomplish a project deliverable, it is easy to start adding more work, generally in support functions, that may or may not be necessary. The project manager must be careful that in the course of conducting work activities, more work is not added that increases cost or creates schedule conflicts to the work directly related to the deliverable.

  The project manager must understand the control of scope is to ensure the minimum required work is being performed to correctly complete the project objective, and the project is limited to *only* the work required and nothing more.

- *Product scope*—One of the most important things the project manager and those evaluating the request of the customer can do at the beginning of a project is to solicit and document as much detailed information that defines the product or service as possible. In many cases, it's difficult for the customer to understand all of the details at the beginning of the project, as the customer may be in the process of developing something, and only after the project has begun will understand more details of the deliverable that must be added or changed throughout the project lifecycle. This is typically handled in two ways:

  - An official change order process is used that allows the customer to change particular items on the fly throughout the project lifecycle. This is an organized form of communication that documents change required on a project deliverable.

- The customer makes small, incremental changes with no official change process and typically through several different channels of communication that add cost and duration to work activities; this is called *scope creep*.

The scope of the product is then defined as the minimum requirement of work that needs to be performed and limited to *only* the work required to complete the project deliverable that meets the customer's expectations.

- **Resource control**—The next area of control where project managers spend a great deal of time is controlling resources used throughout the project lifecycle. As a reminder, resources can be internal to the organization, such as human resources, capital equipment, facilities, and available finances, or contracted equipment or services brought in from outside the organization for use on project activities. At the beginning of a project, when the project manager has broken down the project deliverable into its smallest components, she begins to understand all the resources required within each work activity to produce the intended project deliverable. As this simply produces the list of everything required, it does not necessarily guarantee that the organization has all of these resources and that resources will be available when required throughout the project lifecycle.

As the project manager begins to formulate a plan for what resources are required for each work activity and whether she will use internal or external resources, it becomes evident that there may be areas throughout the project lifecycle where there may be a risk of resources being unavailable, and controls may need to be developed to ensure resources will not be an issue. The project manager can determine at the beginning of the project if the organization has human resources with skills required for each work activity and/or if external resources will be required.

- *Resource allocation control*—One way the project manager can reduce the risk of resource availability is to schedule with internal functional managers the requirement of key resources so these resources will be available when required for project work activities.

  Another resource allocation control tool that can be used is where the project manager can make arrangements to contract external resources at the beginning of the project to ensure those resources will be available when required.

An area of concern in managing resources throughout the project lifecycle is when the project manager finds that resources are not available or will be available at reduced quantity during a specific work activity. This creates a constraining risk, where work may not be completed and the project manager is faced with adding more resources or extending the work activity duration to ensure the deliverable is completed. In some cases, resources are the issue within the organization, and if a particular project has work activities where time duration may not be as important, the project manager can utilize a control tool called *resource leveling* to make adjustments in work activities to utilize resources available.

- *Resource leveling*—One of the most common issues related to project activities is the utilization of resources and how certain resources can present risks in the form of challenges or constraints. Just because resources are identified and scheduled at the beginning of the project, their availability and effective utilization at the time they are required on a work activity may not always go as planned.

  Overutilization and changes in availability of resources are typically the root cause of problems that create either schedule or cost-related issues when work activities need to start. In these cases, the typical response would be to simply add more resources or simply hope the overutilization of resources does not cause excessive problems in regard to employee burn-out.

Resource leveling is a technique that enables the project manager to make adjustments in resource utilization not based on problems with one work activity alone, but taking into consideration several work activities within a particular duration of the project. The project manager can make adjustments in the utilization of resources to level out the number of hours worked per day and the number of resources required per day, per work activity.

Resource leveling is most effective in controlling resource-constrained situations. For example, critical resources are available only at certain times or in reduced quantities; resources have changed to being over-allocated in demand loading; or it is determined that previously scheduled human resources may not have the required skill set. So either additional resources need to be added or skilled resources need to be acquired from other projects or externally. These risks can be typical and common for project managers on all types of projects. One approach in resource leveling is evaluating the activity schedule and overall project schedule to see if additional time on one activity might allow resource leveling. Figure 7.4 illustrates a resource-constrained activity, and Figure 7.5 illustrates how leveling resources would look when more duration is added to the work activity.

Software Engineering Resource Availability																	
Resources	1	2	3	4	5	6	7	8	9	10	11	12	13	14	15	16	17
A. Develop Requirements	RS LSE	RS LSE	RS LSE														
B. Develop Architecture				LSE	LSE	LSE	LSE	LSE									
C. Design Sub-Module A				SE	SE	SE	SE										
D. Design Sub-Module B				SE	SE	SE	SE	SE	SE	SE	SE						
E. Design User Interface				SE	SE	SE	SE	SE	SE	SE	SE						
F. Assemble & Test A & B												TE SE	TE				
G. Final Assembly													TE SE	TE			
H. Final Test															TE SE	TE	
Available Resources: Research Scientist = 1 Lead Software Engineer = 1 Software Engineer = 2 Test Engineer = 1	RS 8 LSE 8	RS 8 LSE 8	RS 8 LSE 8	LSE 8 SE 24	LSE 8 SE 24	LSE 8 SE 24	LSE 8 SE 24	LSE 8 SE 16	SE 16	SE 16	SE 16	TE 8 SE 8	TE 8	TE 8 SE 8	TE 8	TE 8 SE 8	TE8

Figure 7.4 Resource-constrained activity

Resource Requirement after Leveling																			
Resources	1	2	3	4	5	6	7	8	9	10	11	12	13	14	15	16	17	18	19
A. Develop Requirements	RS LSE	RS LSE	RS LSE																
B. Dovolop Architecture				LSE	LSE	LSE	LSE	LSE											
C. Design Sub-Module A				SE	SE														
D. Design Sub-Module B						SE	SE	SE	SE	SE	SE	SE	SE						
E. Design User Interface						SE	SE	SE	SE	SE	SE	SE	SE						
F. Assemble & Test A & B														TE SE	TE				
G. Final Assembly																TE SE	TE		
H. Final Test																		TE SE	TE
Available Resources: Research Scientist = 1 Lead Software Engineer = 1 Software Engineer = 2 Test Engineer = 1	RS 8 LSE 8	RS 8 LSE 8	RS 8 LSE 8	LSE 8 SE 8	LSE 8 SE 8	LSE 8 SE 16	LSE 8 SE 16	LSE 8 SE 16	SE 16	SE 16	SE 16	SE 8	SE 16	TE 8 SE 8	TE 8	TE 8 SE 8	TE8	TE 8 SE 8	TEB

Figure 7.5 Resource leveling, adding more duration

7.4 Manage Change Control

As the project manager manages work performed in each activity, change is inevitable, either through internal process requirements or externally to the organization from the customer or suppliers. Project managers should understand what change is and that in some cases it can be detrimental to a project, while in other cases it can be managed easily, maintaining good customer service and in most cases used in managing risk. The most important component of change is "control," and as long as the project manager has control over change on a project, change can simply be managed as just another project process.

- **Why change?**—Some project managers like the idea of developing a project management plan at the beginning of a project, as this puts them in the driver's seat of control of the project design, such that almost all of the components of a project can be defined, such as the deliverable, project duration, all of the resources required to complete the deliverable, all the costs associated with the project, and all of the individual work activity durations. Once this project plan is been completed, it is plausible to ask why anything should be changed when everything has been defined?

The answer lies with people, and as long as people are associated with projects, change is inevitable. When a customer is trying to decide what type of deliverable to specify for the organization to produce, there are things that have to be included to define that deliverable correctly and accurately. The customer may assume the organization that will produce the deliverable understands certain common industry components and therefore simply does not define them in detail. In other cases, the customer simply forgets to include details or only knows some of the details, and because they are developing something internally themselves, may not have the information available to define certain details until later in the project lifecycle.

When projects have defined all of the procurement requirements, depending on the complexity of certain items that need to be purchased or extremely long time spans between the beginning of the project and when the item will need to be purchased for a work activity, suppliers and vendors may require a change be made to an item when an item is purchased.

Throughout the project lifecycle, the project manager must make changes to work activities such as scheduling, resources that were originally identified that need to be changed because they are no longer available, or internal processes that are updated that require small modifications in work activity.

As we can see, project managers can be faced with several conditions that either require change or present the opportunity for a change that result in an improvement in either the project deliverable or the project cost or schedule. Project managers should develop a process of change that allows changes to be made under a controlled environment because this is not only facilitating change to be made, but reducing or eliminating any risks associated with change.

- **Is change accepting risk?**—As project managers evaluate several different types of change that may be required throughout the project lifecycle, they typically conclude the evaluation with an assessment of what risk is associated with any given change. As the project manager typically likes to define everything in the project management plan at the beginning of a project, it would be accurate to say any change to that original plan will have a risk associated with it. This being the case, why would the project manager approve change, if by association she also has to accept risk?

As we have seen, change is inevitable, either from internal organizational processes or from external customer or supplier requirements. Project managers must understand that they will have to deal with change at some point in a project lifecycle, and that although approving a change might be accepting risk, like any other process in project management, risk can be identified and analyzed, and a response developed. The important aspect of accepting risk in evaluating change is that change will be controlled through a process, and therefore risk can also be controlled through the same process.

- **Change control process**—Like so many other areas of work activity throughout an organization, change control activities are conducted by means of developing and maintaining processes that define each step required in performing a change correctly and efficiently. The way to conduct changes on a project is simply an outline of activities required to implement those changes and therefore can be managed as a process. The only way change can truly be controlled is by developing a change process so that it can be documented and executed with consistency. The project manager can then use this process throughout the project at whatever level required in managing the implementation and measuring the effect that change will have on project work activities.

The four primary steps that make up the process of change include *propose*, *implement*, *communicate*, and *measure*.[1]

- *Propose*
    1. ***Gather data***—The first step in determining whether change is required is to review information gathered from work activities, analyze it for compliance to work activity expectations, and decide whether corrective action is

---

[1] Wilson, Randal. *A Comprehensive Guide to Project Management Schedule and Cost Control: Methods and Models for Managing the Project Lifecycle.* Upper Saddle River, NJ: Pearson, 2014.

required. Changes should always be based on actual data taken from work activities and not from opinions or hearsay of individuals who are not involved directly with the work activity in question. It is important the analysis of information clearly indicates the need for correction and that there is no question as to the validity of what the data indicates.

2. ***Define the need for a specific change***—After it has been determined that correction is needed for a work activity, that information and analysis can be used to develop the details and scope of a proposed change. This step in the change process is important because it summarizes what the data actually indicates in a form that can be understood by those who will be evaluating the need for the change. It is also important to include what the expected outcome will be on activity performance.

3. ***Propose change***—After a need for change has been clearly identified, the change needs to be articulated and presented in the form of a proposal. This can be a short statement outlining details of the change, called a *change order form*, or it can be complex and detailed, requiring a full written proposal outlining all the details, charts, graphs, and other supporting documentation to accurately articulate the scope of change. The proposal's development is the final form indicating the details of how change should be documented and communicated to those evaluating the change for approval.

4. ***Validate and sign-off***—The proposal should be submitted to a team of individuals who are knowledgeable in the work activity such that they can evaluate the information provided in the proposal and determine whether this is an acceptable course of action. It may be determined that offline testing should be required to validate the outcome of a proposed change. In other cases, the opinions of subject matter experts regarding other courses of action may produce a similar outcome with less risk or impact to schedule or cost. After the change has been validated,

it is important that the team sign off on this document to validate that a change has been evaluated and approved; this information can then be communicated in project status updates.

- *Implement*
  1. **Conduct changes**—After a proposed change has been approved, implementation can be a difficult hurdle to get over, depending on the type of change requested. In some cases, there may be resistance because it is common for people to reject change. The reason can be simple fear of the unknown or a lack of details regarding how the proposed change will affect the expected outcome. It is best for the project manager to inform in advance those staff who will be implementing the change so that they can ask questions and details can be conveyed to help them understand how and why a change is being implemented. It is also important for the project manager to convey that work activity performance is noncompliant and that the change is necessary to bring the work activity performance back into compliance to the baseline expectations. The project manager should understand the importance of gaining the trust and the buy-in of resources who are implementing the change, because this can be an important factor in the success of what the change is trying to accomplish.

  2. **Manage scope of change**—The project manager and/or the responsible individuals tasked with implementing the change need to manage the details that define the scope of the change intended. This task is important because those implementing the change may interpret some of the details differently than those who understand the scope of the change more clearly. The change will be successful only if implemented exactly the way it was documented and proposed, so careful management of details during the implementation is critical.

  3. **Publicize changes**—When the implementation process is complete, the project manager and/or responsible

individuals implementing the change should document that all steps have been completed and the process of this change has been verified. This task is important so that staff conducting the work activity and other project staff and stakeholders know when the change has been accomplished. It is important that the change process have a definite completion point so that information gathering and analysis can be documented from that completion point and reflect the impact that the change was designed to make. It may also be a requirement of the change process to have a final sign-off officially validating that the change has been completed.

- *Communicate*

  1. ***Establish who needs to know***—As with the initial group of individuals required to evaluate and sign off the proposal, another group of individuals who have interest in knowing that the change is complete needs to be established. This group may include the original individuals evaluating the proposal but might also include functional managers and executives or other supporting staff who need to know the change has been implemented.

  2. ***Determine appropriate method of communication***—Depending on the type of information used in the original proposal and the information gathered to validate that a change has been completed, individuals receiving this information need to have it in a form that can be easily understood. If the change can be easily articulated in a memo or email, this method can be used for simple forms of communicating work activity status reflecting a change. If a change is more complex and requires a much more detailed and sophisticated proposal, similar levels of detailed information need to be prepared in forms that can be effectively communicated to other individuals. The communication of information may not be within the same location, so other creative forms of communication might have to be used if individuals are in various locations.

- *Measure*

    1. ***Compare to original baseline***—Another important component in the implementation and completion of a change for a work activity is to continue measuring the activity and analyze performance as compared to the original baseline. This step is required to validate a change is actually producing the expected outcome, and work performance is being measured in compliance with the project baseline. With any change, it is required to validate the success of that change or to determine whether other problems were created or the change simply did not produce the expected outcome and should be reversed. It is important to note that simply making the change does not always improve work activity performance and, in some cases, may actually create other problems. It is extremely important the project manager validate that a change produces the expected outcome, because this is the control function she uses to bring work activity performance back into alignment with the project baseline.

    2. ***Determine sustainability***—The last component of the change process needs to be a determination of the sustainability of a change. In some cases, changes have a permanent influence on work activity performance, and the change could be considered permanent and sustainable. In other cases, changes might have a temporary influence, but the ongoing measurement and analysis of data show fluctuations in performance and question the sustainability of the change. This data is very important because the project manager needs to analyze and understand the validity of a change and whether or not that change should be kept in place or reversed. In some cases, a change might simply need some minor alteration to improve its outcome and sustainability. This again points back to the importance of monitoring, gathering, and analyzing data on work activity performance to track any fluctuations or variance in performance after a change has been implemented.

7.5 Project Document Updates

After the project manager has developed monitoring and controls for project activities, it should be documented what monitoring systems and control tools and techniques have been implemented. As the project manager will have documented all of the work activity requirements and the project management plan and developed a risk management plan that documents how to identify, analyze, and respond to risks, the development of risk monitoring and controls are usually completed toward the end of developing the risk management plan. This is due to the requirement of the information being obtained while developing risk management documentation, but it is also included as either separate standalone documents or in the risk management plan document. It is highly advised that the project manager include details of how the risk monitoring and control system were developed, as this can be not only important for other project managers and to create a standard of risk monitoring and control, but used as a training tool for project managers unaware of how to monitor and control risk. The project manager should include details of the monitoring and control system on the following project documents:

- Project management plan
- Risk management plan
- Risk register
- Change request
- Lessons learned document

7.6 Summary

Once the project manager has finished identifying risks, analyzing risk, prioritizing each risk, and developing the risk responses, it is also necessary for her to develop a system of monitoring work activities for signs that problems are imminent. A common technique project managers can use in conjunction with risk responses is to develop early warning sign indicators called triggers that can alert the project manager and project staff that an identified risk is imminent. This is a valuable tool, as it can even give an early warning indication before risk begins, allowing the project manager more options and possibly eliminating a risk before it begins.

This chapter covered several monitoring techniques project managers can use to drive early warning information. As the project manager is not typically involved with all work activities, there will need to be a monitoring system in place to alert the project manager that a risk has occurred so a response can be implemented as quickly as possible.

In addition to establishing a monitoring system for each work activity, the project manager also needs to implement controls that can assist in controlling work activities to prevent problems as well as controlling responses to ensure they are carried out as designed. Common controls for project activities would include quality control for the output deliverable, cost control, manufacturing, engineering statistical process control, schedule controls, and resource controls.

Another area of risk that is common for many projects is managing change that will be inevitable throughout the project lifecycle. As we have seen, change can come in many forms, including human resource changes, specification changes requested by the customer, change as a result of a risk response, and change as a function of conducting procurements. Change, either to improve some aspect of the project or as requested by the customer, is typically seen as a good thing if managed well, and the project manager needs to ensure there is a change management control system in place to effectively and efficiently manage all changes required throughout the project lifecycle. Managing change control is considered another process within the project management plan.

The project manager, in developing a monitoring and control system as well as a change management system, needs to update project documentation to reflect these developments. Typical documents the project manager would update with monitoring and control information are risk register updates, risk management plan, project management plan, work breakdown structure, and the lessons learned document.

The project manager must understand the importance of developing an effective monitoring and control system, as this is required to effectively control risks throughout the project lifecycle. The manager must also understand the importance of managing changes that are required and the risk change can present throughout the project lifecycle without an effective change management plan. These types of tools are proactive approaches the project manager can take to understanding how information can be used to avoid problems before they occur.

7.7 Review Questions

1. Explain the significance of how a monitoring and control system would benefit risk management.
2. Give examples of early warning sign triggers that may be used for a particular risk.
3. List the five major controls used in project work activities and give an example of how to use one control.
4. Explain why change on a project needs to be managed and describe some of the effects of change not being managed on a work activity as well as an organization.
5. What are similar key components found in a change management control process?

7.8 Key Terms

Risk monitoring

Early warning triggers

Risk control

Quality control

Schedule control

Cost control

Scope control

Resource control

Manage change control

7.9 PMBOK Connections (5th Ed.)

11.6 Control Risks

7.10 Case Study (Use for Chapters 7 and 8)

Saltwater Moving Inc. has been contracted to move a large two-story home from one location to another location 12 blocks away. The home will be lifted off of its foundation and mounted on moving equipment and will be taken down a residential street to a main boulevard, requiring closure of the Boulevard for six blocks during the move. Saltwater Moving Inc. performs these types of moves as a primary function of their business, and the project manager spends a great deal of time preparing for a one-time project such as moving a large house.

In developing this project, the project manager has identified many risks related to lifting the house onto moving equipment, and he's scheduled contractors for electrical, phone, and cable utilities to be turned off and cables extending across streets to be removed temporarily to accommodate the path for the house. Plans will be made to contract staff to manage traffic control as well as pedestrian bystanders for safety. Analysis of the structural integrity of the house and the moving equipment having the capability of successfully moving the house to the new location has been performed and determine that there is a 10% probability of catastrophic damage. Once the house has been relocated to the new site, removal of the house from the moving equipment and locating it on the new foundation will require precision accuracy and the cooperation of the building contractor hired to create the new foundation.

7.11 Case Study Questions

1. In the development of the risk monitoring plan, identify top priority risks that would be monitored.
2. Identify any early warning triggers that would assist during this move.
3. Discuss strategies for quality control and resource control on this project.

8

Procurement Monitoring and Control

8.1 Introduction

As the project manager develops the project management plan at the onset of a new project, there are many uncertainties he will be faced with, and how he plans for these uncertainties can have a huge impact on the success of the project. We have already discussed how planning for risk is important, but monitoring and controlling risk throughout the project lifecycle helps reduce or eliminate risks before they happen. This can also be the case where monitoring and controlling procurements are concerned; management of risk can reduce problems associated with managing a project on the whole.

When we think about monitoring and control from a risk standpoint, this is usually performed exclusively by the project manager or any identified project staff assisting in the monitoring control function, given that these activities cross several departments within the organization as well as external suppliers/vendors and subcontractors. When we look at monitoring and control systems integrated into the procurement department, this can be performed by either the project manager or exclusively by the procurement department. It should be noted that when the project manager wishes to develop and implement monitoring and control tools for the procurement department, some individuals in that department may take this as the project manager telling them how to do their jobs. In reality, within most organizations everyone thinks he is doing a great job and resents oversight by someone outside of his department. It's advisable the project manager consult the functional manager over the procurement department for the best implementation of monitoring and control tools.

The warning here for the project manager is to use professionalism and tact when informing the procurement department that monitoring and control tools are needed—that it's simply to reduce the risk of incorrect procurements or cost overruns. Organizations might have a well-staffed procurement department that has its own monitoring and control systems in place to ensure the quality of their work. Other organizations might not be as well staffed, or given the staff they have, do not have monitoring or control processes in place to ensure the quality of procurements. In either case, it is best for the project manager to meet with the functional manager of the procurement department to determine the best course of action in using monitoring and control tools for procurements.

As the project manager is evaluating what procurements need to be monitored, she must think outside the box to ensure every aspect of purchasing related to the project (not just items that are purchased) is evaluated. This can include any subcontractors that are used, rental or lease agreements for equipment or facilities, as well as all purchases required. Some organizations charge projects a square footage fee for occupying a facility, which must be monitored and controlled, as well as any charges for internal specialized resources that would be allocated to project work activities. The project manager must also be mindful that the duration of a project may play a role in procurement activities. When cost estimates are derived in the form of proposals and bids and, in some cases, contracts, there is typically a time frame for guaranteed prices, and if not procured within the timeframe, prices have to be renegotiated. On projects that can span several years, the project manager must understand how the procurement department addresses estimating project costs for items that will need to be procured in the future. This is important for the project manager in trying to understand the overall project cost and budget at completion, as accurate costs may simply not be available and a rough budget estimate must be used.

Throughout the project lifecycle, regardless of the time duration, it is still the responsibility of the project manager, and he will need to have a system in place to monitor and control procurements to help reduce or eliminate risk of cost overruns. This chapter focuses on techniques that can be used in both monitoring and controlling procurement activities.

8.2 Procurement Monitoring Techniques

The project manager spends a great deal of time in the planning stages identifying all procurements required throughout the project, but that is only the first step in ensuring procurements will actually be conducted as anticipated. The second step is, during the course of the project, the project manager must monitor procurements to ensure the purchasing agents fully understand the details regarding each purchase. Purchasing agents must understand that details mean the difference between success and failure, and it only takes missing one detail to purchase an item incorrectly. The purchasing agents have a great responsibility in fully understanding what it is they are to procure, and this is why monitoring the procurements is simply a second set of eyes to ensure, in the best interest of the project, purchases are made correctly. The second reason project managers implement monitoring and controls for procurements is to set up early warning triggers to alert the purchasing agent and project manager of a potential problem. Establishing these early warning triggers requires information not only about the procurement, but in what can go wrong.

- **Information sources for procurement monitoring**—The first step in establishing monitors for procurements is to look at the sources of information that would bring to light not only problems and issues that could create potential risks, but in the early warning signs that can be used as triggers to give the purchasing agent and project manager time to develop an alternate plan. It is also important that when reviewing sources for information regarding purchases and early warning signs of problems, an evaluation of the accuracy and reliability of the information source should be conducted so there will be a higher level of confidence in the information gathered and used.

- *Activity information checklists*—To gain the highest level of detail in what actually needs to be procured within each work activity, the activity information checklist can be used as the ground-level basis of information, outlining everything required in each work activity. The checklist includes not only all the work that will be performed, but all of the resources required, materials needed, and any other details outlining requirements to carry out the work activity. This will be one of the best sources of accurate and detailed information, as these checklists are derived directly from the work breakdown structure and every activity required throughout the project.

   In most cases, the activity information is derived directly from customer requirements and specifications, subject matter expert recommendations, and industry standards where codes and regulations have been considered. The project manager usually tries to gather as much detail as possible to best understand all of the requirements and derive resource, cost, and activity duration estimates. This source would be considered one of the most detailed, accurate, and reliable sources of information to derive procurement monitoring and control.

- *Risk register*—The next area of information that provides details regarding specific procurements and problems associated with specific procurements is the risk register. The project manager and assisting project staff go through all of the work activities and determine risks associated with each activity, and then they make sure it is all documented and prioritized in the risk register. As most of the information regarding risks will have been derived from the activity information checklists, the assessment of problems is especially important and indicates what procurements could bring risk.

- *Procurements management plan*—The procurements management plan is generally a higher-level document outlining the plan of how procurements will be conducted; this document can shed light onto certain areas of procurements that may have potential problems. The procurements management plan can also explain procurement processes that will be used and may also need to be monitored.

- *Project management plan*—The project management plan is also a higher-level document outlining all of the management plans; it too can be considered a source of information that may shed light on potential problems regarding procurements throughout the project lifecycle. Using a higher-level document allows for the project manager to have a broader scope of understanding of the entire project and may identify procurement risks from this perspective. In some cases, a decision made for procurement in one part of the project may actually introduce a risk at another part of the project that the project manager would not have seen if not looking at a bigger picture. This would be valuable information not only in setting up monitoring, but in the control of procurements from a strategic standpoint.

- *Accounting*—One of the areas common to the procurement department is where the financial resources come from to conduct procurements: the accounting department. If the project manager wants to obtain information regarding the practices and procedures of the procurement department as well as historical pricing and any problems associated with suppliers/vendors or subcontractors, the accounting department would have the most accurate information. As the procurement department initiates the front-end component of a purchase or issuance of a contract, it's the accounting department that usually picks up the back end in issuing the payments and ensuring the financial conditions of agreements have been met. The accounting department can usually give information regarding potential risks with certain suppliers/vendors and subcontractors that will help the project manager design monitoring controls for these types of procurements.

- *Other project managers*—Another source of valuable information regarding the procurements department, as well as suppliers/vendors and subcontractors, are other project managers within the organization. As project managers complete each project, over the course of time they see a pattern of performance either internally with other departments and resources or externally with suppliers/vendors and subcontractors. It is highly advised that project managers conduct surveys of other project managers' experiences with the procurement department, as well as suppliers/vendors and subcontractors, because there can be a wide variety of information the surveys might yield.

This type of information can give the project manager a different perspective of potential risks relative to procurements that could not have been gained in the activity information checklists, risk register, and other sources that have been used. Care must be taken to accept the information that is given from other project managers, but know that this information, although valuable, may be subjective based on each project manager's relationship with the procurement department and any suppliers/vendors or subcontractors that may be discussed.

- *Lessons learned documentation*—Another important source of information the project manager can always find useful is lessons learned documentation from previous projects. Hopefully the organization has established a culture where project managers document lessons learned on their projects that can be used on future projects to avoid issues and exploit successful tactics. The project manager can see prior purchases, activities conducted by the procurement department, strategies taken in contract negotiation, as well as any purchase pricing, quality, or shipping and delivery issues from various suppliers/vendors and subcontractors.

  It is also helpful when project managers who have used certain human resource subcontractors on projects include comments as to the subcontractors' general attitude, work ethic, quality of work, and pricing, as this can shed light on possible monitoring and control. Depending on the type of contracts that are used with subcontractors, information can be derived from a lessons learned document that would indicate early warning triggers that can be used under certain conditions with certain contractors. In most cases, the lessons learned documents can be valuable sources of information the project manager can use not only in the development of a project, but in the course of conducting all the project activities throughout the project lifecycle.

- **Develop early warning sign triggers**—After the project manager has evaluated sources of information regarding risks that would pertain to procurements throughout the project lifecycle, further evaluation of each risk may reveal slight changes in conditions prior to a risk that may indicate a problem is imminent. These early warning signs can be documented with each risk and are used on each project work activity as triggers to indicate a potential procurement problem. Because these early warning signs are specific to each risk and the conditions surrounding the procurement, very specific information must be derived and can be found in some of the following documentation:

  - *Activity information checklists*—Reviewing documents that have the most detailed information requiring all work that is performed within an activity and likewise any procurements specific to that work activity usually points back to the activity information checklist. This document is useful not only in understanding the conditions for each procurement, but in the events leading up to a procurement, which may indicate a change may be required to avoid an incorrect procurement. The project manager can see the activities leading up to a procurement requirement and can develop a trigger based on information that would suggest a particular item to be purchased is at risk.

  - *Contracts and lease agreements*—If contracts and lease agreements are used, early warning signs can be used to avoid risk, such as a change in conditions prior to the signing of a contract or lease agreement that would alter what is required in the contract or lease agreement, or early warning signs during a contract or lease agreement period that would indicate potential problems. In most cases, the use of early warning signs prior to signing a contract or lease agreement are useful in procurements to avoid risks such as selecting the wrong subcontractor, contracts that may include verbiage that is not in the best interest of the project, or lease agreements for items that are incorrect or no longer needed.

Early warnings may simply be checkpoint reminders for the project manager and purchasing agents to double-check procurements before they are made, or they can actually be results of conversations, information in emails, or any other form of information that would suggest a problem may be imminent with a proposed contract or lease agreement.

- *Work breakdown structure (WBS)*—Used by the project manager to not only understand the breakdown of a project deliverable into it smallest components, but also the organization of each work activity establishing a process in how a deliverable is to be completed. Having established the organization of work activities, the project manager can use this also to develop early warning triggers for critical procurements. The WBS can be used to schedule or trigger early review of critical procurements to ensure all parameters are still correct to avoid an incorrect procurement, as well as a monitoring tool to see if activities prior to critical procurements have developed slight alterations that may change the requirement of a procurement.

- *Procurements management plan*—As we have seen that very detailed information relative to each procurement is important to develop early warning sign triggers, it is also important for the project manager to step back and look at the bigger picture to see if more obvious early warning triggers can be seen from a higher vantage point. There may be conditions early in the project that, if changed, might alter a procurement requirement further along in the project, and this would not be recognized without the project manager looking at a bigger picture.

- *Lessons learned documents*—Again, the lessons learned documents can be useful in designing early warning triggers as the project manager can review completed work activities that required similar procurements and can see conditions leading up to a procurement that may indicate an early warning trigger. The project manager can also see where early warning triggers were successfully used in the past, and can also see where procurements were made incorrectly but conditions prior to the procurement, if monitored, would have indicated a change was required. Lessons learned documents are valuable sources of information if project managers are keeping accurate notes and recording comments based on both successes and failures.

• **Monitoring tools**—When developing monitoring tools that can be used to monitor procurements, the goal is to gather information on what procurements are intended, any contracts or lease agreements that have been developed, and any other procurement-related item that is scheduled to be conducted. This information can be used to evaluate procurements before they happen and give the project manager or the procurements agent time to make adjustments or changes if needed to ensure procurements will be conducted correctly. Common procurement monitoring tools can include

  • *Planned procurement monitor*—This is a document generally developed by the project manager and used by the procurement department as a communication tool that lists what procurements are scheduled on a weekly or monthly basis. This document can be produced by the project manager based on the work breakdown structure and given to the procurement department, or it can be developed by the procurements department if they know what procurements are planned throughout the project.

  The planned procurement monitor is a powerful tool used between the project manager and procurement department. It is typically communicated and reviewed on a weekly basis, generally in status meetings, and can be updated and discussed as needed at any time to reflect changes. An example of a planned procurement monitor is shown in Figure 8.1.

Planned Procurement Monitor								
	Purchases				Contracts			
Activity	Item Desc	Order Date	Due Date	Actual Delivery Date	Sub Contractor	Activity Task	Required Date	Finish Date

Figure 8.1 Planned procurement monitor

- *Contract review and approval process*—Another important monitoring tool that is used where the project manager and purchasing agents, as well as any other organizational staff or management that may be required, can review contracts and lease agreements prior to being issued. As contracted lease agreements can present all kinds of challenges once entered into, it is advisable that the project manager and purchase agent review a contract or lease agreement to ensure the deliverable being called out is correct in all required detail. They also confirm the supplier/vendor or subcontractor has been approved, and any special condition verbiage has been evaluated along with a level of risk determined and approved.

- *Work activity status meetings*—Conducted frequently, in some cases daily, but in most cases weekly and yields more specific information as to the progress of work activities and can shed light on any changes or adjustments that may be required on future procurements. It is important the project manager review the plan procurements monitor document in the activity status meeting, so planned procurements can be discussed and any changes can be evaluated, approved, and included on the planned procurement monitor document. Weekly status meetings can also reveal changes that may need to be made in obtaining a subcontractor prior to issuing a contract.

8.3 Procurement Control Techniques

As the project manager monitors procurements, situations will arise that require control or changes with regard to procurement activities. The project manager, having the responsibility to ensure the procurement process is being conducted correctly for her project, needs to establish two very important processes—*procurement control* and *procurement change*. With regard to procurement control, it is important to remember that the project manager is not telling procurement personnel how to do their jobs, but confirming that in doing their jobs, what they are procuring is correct.

- **What is procurement control?**—When project managers are responsible to ensure procurements are being conducted correctly, this can include overseeing what procurements are conducted, managing relationships, and monitoring performance of suppliers/vendors and subcontractors, as well as managing any change required with purchases, subcontractor contracts, and the lease agreements. Procurement control requires not only the development of all required procurements within the project, but the monitoring of all procurement activities to ensure procurements are being conducted correctly.

- **Purchase and contract control**—The project manager is typically responsible to inform the procurements department of all procurements requirements for his project. In doing so, the project manager is also responsible to control procurements by ensuring they are conducted correctly and manage any changes that come up. The project manager can utilize some of the techniques used in monitoring purchases, which can include

  - *Planned procurement monitor*—Used by the project manager for not only monitoring procurements, but also in controlling all procurements due to the fact that this document is reviewed regularly by the project manager and communicated on a regular basis between the project manager and the procurement department. This document allows the project manager to ensure procurements are made correctly and any updates or changes have been incorporated prior to procurement being conducted. This is one of the most powerful tools the project manager can use in both monitoring and controlling procurements, as it can have the latest and most accurate information, allowing both the project manager and the procurements department to be on the same page at all times with pending procurements.

- *Contract review and approval process*—Another monitoring tool that can be used as a control tool that allows the project manager and purchasing agent to review contracts and lease agreements before they are issued. This is also a powerful tool used as a stopgap measure. Because contracts and lease agreements are often legal and binding, every effort must be made to ensure not only that the correct contractors have been selected, but that the deliverable has been evaluated as being correct and all detail required and any conditions and associated risks have been acknowledged or approved. This is used as a control function to help ensure the project and organization are only engaged in contracts necessary for project work activity and at a risk level the project and organization are willing to accept.

- *Contract type*—Can be used to control procurements where subcontractors or lease agreements will be required for project work activities. As previously discussed in this book, there are several types of contracts that can be selected based on how the organization wants to control price structure as well as risk. As contracts can be negotiated, and pricing established, these work as effective control mechanisms because in many cases contracts can be negotiated at the beginning of a project, giving the project manager more peace of mind since the procurements part of acquiring the contractor has already been established. Contracts are also good for managing payment to ensure the organization is fulfilling their side of the agreement.

- *Procurement performance reviews*—Another tool the project manager can use to assess the procurements department's performance in conducting procurements for their project. Performance reviews typically include the evaluation of items, such as the performance of various suppliers/vendors and subcontractors, quality audits for products delivered or work performed, and general assessment of the relationship. Performance reviews can also include the evaluation of the procurement department's performance in timely and accurate purchases, attention to detail with critical purchases, and effective communication with suppliers/vendors and subcontractors as well as project staff.

- *Inspections and audits*—Can be used by the project manager and/or procurement department to verify supplier/vendor or subcontractor performance. These inspections can include quality of product or work performed, attention to critical details, and on-time delivery of a product or deliverable.

- *Accounting department*—Can evaluate payments that are made after verification of delivery or satisfactory work performed and any disputes regarding pricing or payments to suppliers/vendors or subcontractors. Accounting might also be aware of any returns, disputes, or legal actions that have been issued that the project manager and purchasing department should be aware of.

8.4 Integrated Procurement Change Control

In addition to control of procurement, project managers also need to control changes with regard to procurements throughout the project lifecycle. As changes are inevitable with items that have to be purchased, work performed by subcontractors, and equipment or facilities that will have to be leased, the important aspect of this area of procurement is to control change. As with many other aspects of project management, the best way to manage change is to have a process that organizes information, defines the change, and controls how change is conducted and implemented. In the case of contracts and the lease agreements, terms and conditions may be included that dictate how change will be managed, if allowed at all. With all other procurements, a change control process is required to effectively and efficiently manage and control change.

- **Change control process**—The project manager, in developing a change control process, should seek the advice of other project managers and organizational upper management as to the availability of an existing process the organization has already developed. It is incumbent on the project manager to ensure they are consistent with pre-established organizational processes. Some organizations have a formal Project Management Office (PMO) in which project management processes, documents, and templates are created, managed, and controlled. If the organization does not have a PMO or any established change control process, the change control process outlined in Chapter 7, "Risk Monitoring and Control," can be used to manage changes required in conducting procurement.

- **Supplier/vendor orders**—When changes are required that involve orders placed with suppliers or vendors, the project manager and purchasing agent must understand under what conditions change will be allowed. If the project manager has an integrated monitoring system in place for procurement, changes are incorporated before orders are made, thus eliminating the requirement to notify the supplier or vendor to change an order. In this scenario, the project manager will have control over what change will be required and approve modifications to a purchase before it is placed.

  In the case where procurement has already placed an order and a change must be made, this may or may not be achievable and depends on when the order was placed and when the change was identified. Most suppliers and vendors, having received an order, typically begin the process of fulfilling that order as quickly as possible. Many factors can play a role as to whether an order can be changed at all:

  - Changes cannot be made after an order has been placed as a fundamental condition of the order.

  - Changes can be made if identified quickly after the order is placed and if items purchased are simply stock items and the supplier or vendor allows changes after the placement of an order. This would be a condition where a stocked item once pulled to fulfill the order, can simply be put back in stock and the correct item can be pulled. This condition will only be available if the change can be made before items are shipped.

- If the supplier is a manufacturer and the purchased item has to be created, changes are typically not allowed because the supplier will have a build request in place and will start procuring materials and preparing production quickly after the order is been placed, making a change virtually impossible.

- **Subcontractor contracts**—When changes are required where subcontractors are being used, change is typically allowed and managed under a change control process. Subcontractors are used to create something or perform a service, and if the subcontractor is notified of the change in advance, negotiations can be made to accommodate the change. As most contracts define in detail what the deliverable from the contractor will be, the contract stipulates if all the conditions of that deliverable are met, the buyer will agree to the compensation documented in the agreement. If the buyer requests a change of some form in the deliverable, that change must be documented, evaluated by the contractor as to its feasibility, a price and timeframe negotiated, and a change order produced. The change must also be approved by both parties. This change order is generally in addition to the terms of the contract and in some cases added to the contract or included as a separate document (contract) with its own terms and payment structure.

In controlling these types of change, contractors using a fixed contract or cost reimbursable contract may require a separate change order contract to manage any changes in the deliverable, making it more difficult for the contractor in allocating resources for the added work and ensuring payment is fair and equitable. These types of contracts usually place more risk on the contractor and help protect the buyer. If a time and materials contract is used, changes to the deliverable are much easier, as they are simply added to the statement of work and whatever time and materials are required are billed by the contractor. As the contractor can accept additions and changes easily, you can also add materials easily that may be more difficult to control by the buyer. This type of contract favors the contractor in accumulating more work and ensuring payment for added time and material, while increasing the risk assumed by the buyer because the time required by the contractor may be difficult to control.

8.5 Project Document Updates

After the project manager has established controls and is both monitoring and controlling procurements, she should update various project documents to record what control tools have been implemented. It is important the project manager record control systems that have been designed and used, as this needs to be communicated to other project staff and the procurement department. In addition to communicating these updates, depending on the organizational structure, the project manager might have to seek approval to use certain controls under certain conditions. The project manager might also want to review these documents in the future to refresh her memory as to what controls were successful so they can be used on future projects.

As always, the project manager should be recording things like the use of controls in the lessons learned document as to their success or failure in providing procurement control. The lessons learned document is not only valuable for the project manager to review on future projects, but is useful for other project managers and can be used as a training tool for new project managers to take advantage of valuable processes, tools, and techniques that have been used in the past. Some of the documents that need to be updated to reflect procurement control tools and techniques may include

- Project management plan
- Procurement management plan
- Activity information checklist
- Change request
- Lessons learned documents

8.6 Summary

Much like managing risks in project work activities, conducting procurements can have many items in process at any given time, and generally there is an associated risk with each item. As we know, conducting procurement can itself produce risks for project work activities, and the project manager must also develop monitoring and control techniques to ensure procurements are being conducted correctly.

As with monitoring risks, there also can be early warning sign triggers established to monitor all purchases and contracts for early signs of problems. This technique has proven effective for project managers and purchasing agents to catch a piece of information that would have generated an incorrect purchase or a devastating term or condition or specification call out in a contract. Monitoring tools are also valuable for project updates to ensure changes have been implemented before purchases are made.

The project manager, in conjunction with the purchasing agent, also establishes procurement controls that are actually put in place to protect purchases and contract agreements and avoid errors that can cause potential risks. The unfortunate area with procurements is if something has been purchased incorrectly, the project management clock is ticking. If procurement is correct and products delivered on schedule, everything's fine; if it is incorrect items will have to be returned, and time will be spent waiting for new ones to be shipped. This type of error typically generates project delays that impact the schedule and in some cases the budget. Controls designed to ensure purchases are double-checked and contracts are evaluated is one more level of insurance the project manager can have in trying to avoid procurement risks that can also lead to schedule and budget issues.

Another important area of control is managing change required in procurement. This can be anything from having a new purchasing agent assigned to the project to finding out that an item is no longer available and something slightly different will have to be used. In some cases, internal requirements have generated a change of procurement, while in other cases external requirements might have required change in not only procurement but contract agreements. The project manager must ensure there is a change management process in place designed for procurement, as this will be an effective tool for control.

The project manager must also update project documents to reflect any type of monitoring and control techniques that are being used, as well as a procurement change management plan. The procurement management plan, project management plan, risk management plan, activity information checklist, and the lessons learned document are all examples of documents that can be used to reflect what is being implemented to manage and control procurement.

8.7 Review Questions

1. If purchases are being conducted in what would seem to be a controlled atmosphere, why is monitoring controls needed in the procurement department relative to a project?

2. Give an example of an early warning sign trigger that could be identified for an item purchased for a project work activity.

3. Discuss various controls that can be implemented for the use of contract agreements.

4. Explain a technique that can be used to manage change requirements with subcontractors.

8.8 Key Terms

Procurement monitoring

Procurement control

Change requests

Early warning triggers

Integrated procurement change control

Activity information checklist

8.9 PMBOK Connections (5th Ed.)

12.3 Control Procurements

8.10 Case Study Questions (Use Case Study in Chapter 7)

1. Discuss any procurement monitoring that would be implemented for either purchases or contracts on the project in the case study in Chapter 7.

2. What contract controls might be implemented for the contractors used in this case study?

3. Would there be any early warning triggers that can be identified concerning contractors used in this case study?

4. Given the move of this house is occurring on a single day, yet the preparation for this move might take several months, explain how change processes might be managed leading up to and including the day of the move.

Part IV
Project Closer

Projects are comprised of several work activities that are all used in the development of a project deliverable; each activity has a start and a finish, and all items required of that activity must be completed in order for the next activity to begin. We typically think of the things required for a work activity as the resources needed to carry out tasks of the work activity, the allocation of time required by resources for the duration of a work activity, finances required to fund everything within the work activity, and all of the departments that are peripheral to the project that will supply supporting efforts. When all work is completed, the project manager and any assisting staff evaluate all work to ensure it is been completed correctly, which is called closing work activities.

As the project manager performs several types of actions that will close out various aspects of the work activity, two important aspects need to be evaluated to ensure they have been closed out correctly: closing risk events and closing procurements. It is important the project manager realize that although problems may have happened in the course of a work activity and responses were initiated, it might not always be clear if what was designed in the response was completely finished or closed out. It is also important that the manager know that the procurements department, which was responsible for many purchases and contracts throughout the work activity, will also need to be evaluated to ensure all conditions have been met and procurements can be finalized and closed. Chapter 9, "Close Risk Events," and Chapter 10, "Close Procurements," cover details on how project managers can close out risk events and all procurements for their projects.

9

Close Risk Events

9.1 Introduction

Project managers will more than likely have to respond to risks of some kind on each work activity they manage. Some of these risks may be more complicated than others, and the response designed for each risk can be equally as complex or simple. When a response has been initiated, there can be a variety of things required in the response, and the project manager or owner of the risk response must carry out all requirements and the corresponding responses. Some responses may be simple, such as a task that needs to be carried out by an individual that, once completed, can be considered closed, having effectively addressed the risk; some responses may be very complex, requiring several individuals engaged in a variety of different tasks (for example, rental agreements for items required for a temporary fix, such as renting a large tent to cover a work area due to poor weather). As the task in the activity is completed and work can resume on remaining tasks in the activity without the need of a tent, the response for this risk is still not closed out because the tent needs to be returned and the rental agreement closed.

This is a simple illustration of when a risk event is not necessarily closed, and the project manager or owner of the risk needs to ensure that *everything* required in the response has been completed and finalized. This chapter focuses on techniques to ensure risk events have been properly closed to avoid the risk response itself causing more problems.

9.2 Evaluate Risks

As the project manager begins a new work activity, he is engaged in making sure everything that is required for that work activity will begin as scheduled, resources will be available, procurements have been conducted, and risk owners have been notified that the activity will begin—and the project staff will be watching for early warning triggers. As the work activity progresses and tasks are being completed, if a risk event that was identified never actually happens, that risk can be classified as no longer a threat and is considered closed. There may be special circumstances within the activity that cause the risk to still be considered a threat (although the risk is no longer a tangible threat) until the entire work activity has been completed.

Once a work activity has been completed, the project manager and project staff need to evaluate the activity to ensure everything required has been completed and there remains no threat of any risk events occurring. To ensure that nothing is left in a work activity that would allow a risk event to occur, the project manager should address some basic areas of the work activity:

- **Are project activities completed?**—The project manager needs to evaluate all of the actual work to make certain project objectives were met for those activities. This can include inspection of any deliverable or service, interviews with human resources performing the tasks, or the outcome of discussions within any project status meetings. The project manager must be assured that the work activity was successful in completing the objective, and everything in the work activity can be closed so the project can advance to the next work activity. This can also include all work required by subcontractors for specific tasks within the work activity and confirming compliance of the requirements of the contract. As most of the risks are associated with tasks and procurements within a work activity, it is important the project manager properly close everything within the work activity to avoid any problems moving to the next work activity.

- **Have all responses been completed?**—When the project manager is confident all work activity has been completed and no further actions are required, she turns her attention to any risk responses or contingencies that were initiated in the course of the work activity. The project manager should be aware of any responses that were initiated due to risks that occurred; these should have been clearly communicated among the project manager, owner of the risk, and any other project staff or management that would be involved in a particular risk occurring.

The project manager should review all actions that were taken for each risk response so she can evaluate the effectiveness of each response; this evaluation may include

- Owner of the risk was timely in initiating the response.
- Owner of the risk noted that early warning triggers were effective.
- Notations by the owner of the risk as to the effectiveness of the response.
- Notations by the owner of the risk as to the effectiveness of communication that was designed in the response for other project staff and management.
- Notations by the owner of the risk as to anything that can be improved for this particular response.

After the project manager has performed the evaluation of all risk responses, she can determine if any further actions are required or certify that all actions have been completed and the risk response can be considered closed. This is an important step, as the project manager will be certifying that the response was effective and any actions required in the response have been completed. If actions are still open and left unattended due to the attention of the project team moving toward the next work activity, this can create more problems and may in fact have as big an impact as the original risk it was trying to mitigate or eliminate. It is important the project manager understand that all tasks associated with a risk response be completed and terminated before the project should move to the next work activity.

- **Are procurements completed?**—When evaluating the completion of risk responses, one primary area of concern the project manager should have is whether any actions that were required by procurements may still be left open. In many cases, a response to a risk may have required the purchase of something, perhaps including a contract or lease agreement, and although the item procured was simply required for risk response, it should be treated the same as any procurement for regular work activity requirements. Depending on the risk response, this could actually become complex due to what was required in the risk response, and care must be taken by the project manager to ensure procurements are completed and closed.

  This can also be an area of concern because open procurements left unattended can create bigger problems than the original risk. The project manager must ensure that these procurements are closed out properly to protect the project from its own risk responses. The project manager should work closely with the procurements department to understand any open procurements relative to risk responses and what requirements there are to close out so the project can proceed to the next work activity.

9.3 Close Risk Responses

As the project manager is evaluating all aspects of a work activity and what is required to close out any items remaining open, he must look at a risk response as an opened item and determine what has transpired in the course of a risk response and take action to complete any remaining items. In closing a risk response, there are five primary steps to take to ensure a risk response has been properly closed:

- **Determine what responses are still open**—The first step is determining what risks occurred, what responses were implemented, and what responses still have actions that have not been closed. The project manager can review the risk register to see what risks occurred and what responses were implemented. If the risk register being used does not track risks that actually occurred, the project manager may have to contact the owners assigned to each risk associated with that work activity as to whether their risk occurred.

This is also a good opportunity to interview the risk owner as to the status of a response that was implemented and to find out if all actions have been completed or not. As the risk owners are typically responsible for seeing that all of the requirements of the response are carried out, they would also know if any of these actions have not been completed. The project manager may also solicit information from individuals involved with the work activity that may have knowledge of a risk occurrence and whether response actions are still open. The project manager must use all resources available to understand not only what risks occurred, but what response actions were carried out and if all actions have been completed so the response can be considered closed.

- **Conduct risk response audit**—The second step in closing a risk response is to conduct the risk response audit. To properly close a risk response, an audit must be conducted to ensure that the intended goal of the response was realized and the completion of all response actions was carried out. The project manager or risk owner can conduct the risk response audit using the following steps:
  - Review initial record of potential risk located in the risk register.
  - Confirm owner assigned to the risk.
  - Confirm a risk response was designed for the risk being audited.
  - Interview individuals associated with the risk and solicit comments regarding:
    - How the risk occurred.
    - Was the response initiated by the early warning trigger or the actual risk?
    - How long the risk existed before the response was initiated.

- The effectiveness of the response.
- Final results in correcting the problem.
- Determine effectiveness of risk response.
- **Close response action items**—The project manager and owner of the risk verify that
  - All actions required for the response have been completed.
  - All procurements have been closed out.
  - No remaining resources needed.

  After these steps have been completed, all actions that were taken have been completed, and the project manager and risk owner are confident no further actions are required, verification of response effectiveness can then be completed.

- **Verify response effectiveness**—The project manager and owner of the risk, if one was assigned, assesses all of the information gathered concerning the risk and all actions taken in response to the problem, and then evaluates how effective the response actually was in meeting the goal of the response. The response cannot be considered closed until the effectiveness of the response has been determined and no further actions are required. It's important to note for the project manager and owner of the risk that simply because a response was initiated and completed does not mean it accomplished the goal the response was designed for. In some cases, a response was initiated and completed, and the effects of a risk were still being felt by the work activity.

  A response will have specific actions that, when taken, are designed for a specific outcome, and if that outcome is not accomplished, that response may need to be modified or simply terminated and another response initiated. In a best case scenario, a risk response is initiated and carried out in its entirety and accomplishes the goal it was intended for, resulting in mitigation or elimination of the risk and any impact that risk might have on the project work activity. In either case, a response has a start and a stop, and all actions required in the response must be terminated so the response can be considered closed.

- **Communicate results of response**—The final step in closing out a risk response is to record and communicate the results of the response so other project staff, functional managers, and upper management will know that a particular problem was solved on the project. This type of communication allows the project manager to show that project management processes such as designing responses for risk actually are successful and are a valuable use of time at the beginning of the project in developing a risk management plan. It is also important the results of a risk response are communicated to others involved in the project team to ensure any and all actions required for the risk response were appreciated and are in fact completed so the response can be classified as closed. The project manager should always exercise good communication skills that allow for information such as the results of risk responses to be communicated to the appropriate individuals to show the project is being managed correctly.

9.4 Claims and Disputes

An important element in closing out risk events and work activities is when claims or disputes are made concerning actions taken during the course of a response that need to be addressed before the response can be closed. Claims and disputes might have been raised in the course of work activities, services that were rendered, or procurements that were made that raise a possible risk of having an impact to the work activity. In most cases, claims and disputes are initially taken through the procurements department or a customer service department and may not always be visible by the project manager or project staff. As these claims and disputes exist for a variety of different reasons, generally resulting from something related to a work activity, some of these claims and disputes may be a result of actions taken from a risk response and need to be addressed by the project manager and risk owner to effectively close a risk response. If the claim or dispute is associated with an open action required from a risk response, the project manager typically uses the same process that the procurement department or customer service department would use to deal with a claim or dispute. The project manager and risk owner evaluating a risk response may need to address the following items concerning a claim or dispute before the risk responses can be closed:

- **Identify claim or dispute**—If the claim or dispute was generated based on an action taken as a risk response, the project manager, or owner of the risk, needs to assess what the claim or dispute is centered around. If an action was taken that created a problem for another department internal to the organization, the functional manager of that department needs to agree upon a resolution with the project manager or risk owner. If the claim or dispute was with an external entity, the project manager or risk manager may need to solicit the help of the procurement department and possibly any other department that may assist in resolving the dispute before the risk response can be closed. Having a claim or dispute outstanding as a function of a risk response does not allow for that response to be closed until the dispute is resolved.

- **Close claims and disputes**—Having outstanding items within a risk response, such as a claim or dispute, does not allow for the response to be closed and therefore makes it difficult to close the work activity. If a condition in the claim or dispute creates alternate actions that may affect the work performed, this can create even more problems for the project manager in completing that activity. It is incumbent on the project manager or risk owner to quickly identify the claim or dispute and work to resolve the issue. Once the project manager or owner of the risk has reached a resolve, the claim or dispute can then be closed, allowing for the risk response to be closed as well. It's important this process is carried out completely, as the project manager cannot afford further problems as a result of risk responses that did not play out well. It's the responsibility of the project manager to ensure all actions, such as risk responses and even claims or disputes as a result of a response, have been taken care of so the project work activity can be officially closed and the project can move to the next work activity.

9.5 Documentation and Communication

Once the project manager has successfully closed all risk responses and verified the outcome of each response is important, the project manager records what has transpired in other project management documentation. The risk register would be the most important project management document that would need to be updated, showing how the response was implemented, the effect of the response, and any challenges or constraints in conducting the actions of the response. This is important information to document, as it not only states what actually happened concerning a particular risk, but this information can be available for review and used at a later date by other project managers.

Documenting information such as risk responses and how effective the response strategy was is extremely valuable. This information in project documentation not only serves to archive this information with the project artifacts, but it can be communicated during the project to other project staff, functional managers, and upper management as to the success of risk response strategies. As project managers design responses for various risks, they can review these documents to see what worked well in the past and to avoid mistakes that were made. In some cases, even the smallest details within a response strategy can mean the difference of success or failure in what the response intended to accomplish. Over time, project managers within a particular organization who may see similar risks repeated on projects can become very good at being prepared for these risks based on prior experience, and they can therefore build in a cost, schedule, and quality control tool. The following would be typical documents in which information regarding risk responses could be included:

- Risk register
- Risk management plan
- Activity information checklist
- Procurements management plan
- Lessons learned document

9.6 Summary

Various processes must be performed within the final processing of a risk management plan; unfortunately one that is underestimated, if completed at all, is closing out risk events. Much of the planning for risk has to do with the proactive approach in understanding what can happen, developing a response, monitoring activities for early signs of problems, and implementing a responsive required—but there is a final step in ensuring that all actions carried out in a response have been completed.

Risk responses are designed to accomplish a particular objective in mitigating or eliminating a potential risk, but all too often little is done to ensure that the actions taken accomplished the goal. The first step is to assess any responses that have been conducted and evaluate what activities were carried out to ensure they were completed. The project manager can then determine if the activities were successful in accomplishing the goal. An assessment will need to be made at this point to determine if further action is required or if the risk response was successful in mitigating or eliminating the potential risk.

The next step is to take inventory of all responses that are still being carried out and responses that appear to be finished, in order to assess what steps are remaining. The project manager must determine if more actions are required and review what has to happen to accomplish the goal of the response. Effectively closing a risk response means ensuring actions have been completed, the response accomplished the goal, and any actions or procurements required for the response have been completed and closed out. The project manager must ensure that a risk response is officially closed to ensure there is no remaining effects of the risk that can continue to impact the project.

In the course of carrying out tasks within a work activity, there may be disputes or claims against the organization that will need to be settled to avoid creating a larger problem than already exists. This is typical with the use of contract agreements where there may be disputes or legal claims that will need to be addressed before a work activity can be completed. This may also be the case with items that have been purchased and need to be returned as being incorrect or damaged. This process can take time, and the project manager must understand that the risk of an incorrect procurement can linger on for long periods of time if not dealt with quickly and closed. In some cases, legal action might have been taken that has no real effect to a work activity or the project in general, but was initiated from a dispute in a contract and will be taken up by other departments within the organization. The project manager must ensure that risk responses have been closed and any actions as a result of her response have been completed and assessed as to their effectiveness before the project can close a work activity.

Like any other process within the project, the project manager will want to document closing risk responses, as this will be important for not only the project, but the organization to know that problems were dealt with and completed and the project can move on without further incident.

9.7 Review Questions

1. Discuss what is meant by closing a risk event.
2. Do all risks that were identified need to be closed, or just the ones that have a response that has been implemented?
3. What affects can claims and disputes have on a project or an organization?
4. How would the project manager know when a risk response has been closed?

9.8 Key Terms

Evaluate risks

Close risk responses

Claims and disputes

Risk register

Procurement management plan

Risk management plan

Activity information checklist

9.9 PMBOK Connections (5th Ed.)

11.6 Control Risks

9.10 Case Study (Use for Chapters 9 and 10)

Saltwater Entertainment Inc. was contracted to manage an outdoor concert venue in a large stadium. This required months of planning, which included performers and bands that were contracted to perform throughout the course of a weekend, advertisements and posters, radio and television, the acquisition of the stadium for the duration of one weekend, and the contracting of employees to manage concessions and ticket sales over the course of the weekend. Saltwater Entertainment employs their own staff to set up stage equipment and perform lighting and sound management for all of the performers. They did use external contractors for perimeter security and stage security as well as traffic control. Saltwater Entertainment also contracted a local hotel to manage all of the performers' and Saltwater Entertainment staff housing requirements through the weekend. Saltwater Entertainment contracted transportation for entertainers and Saltwater Entertainment staff to and from the hotel each day.

Most of the weekend went fairly well, but there have been issues that will need to be dealt with in finishing this entertainment project. The following contract conditions will need to be assessed for final closure of all procurements:

1. Two performers have not been paid for performance contracts that they fulfilled. All other performers have been paid.
2. All advertising contracts have fulfilled their requirements in producing the agreed-upon advertising.
3. The transportation company has filed a dispute claiming the interior of one of the transportation vans required excessive cleaning and will not return the deposit. The transportation contract did not stipulate any terms or conditions based on an objective opinion of cleanliness of the transportation vehicles.

4. Hotel staff have reported several rooms having excess cleaning requirements, and they are threatening legal action if not reimbursed. The terms of the hotel agreement clearly state that excessive cleaning requirements will be billed if necessary.

5. It was determined that two of the 16 security guards hired to monitor the perimeter of the stadium were found sitting in their cars for several hours.

9.11 Case Study Questions

1. Identify the primary risks in this case study.

2. Discuss how the closure of these five risk events might be accomplished.

3. Discuss how the type of contract can benefit the buyer in each of the five open contract situations.

10

Close Procurements

10.1 Introduction

Throughout the course of the project lifecycle and depending on the size and complexity of a project, procurements almost always play a part. As each work activity is completed, the process of ensuring every procurement has been finalized, all conditions have been met, and payments have been completed is called *closing procurements*. Projects are usually structured using several different project management processes as well as organizational process assets that determine how projects are structured and managed. As many of these processes are important and need to be carried out in a structured and organized fashion, the area of procurements is one of the most important, but, unfortunately, it is an area that many project managers leave for other individuals in the organization to deal with.

Conducting procurements for project work activities has resulted in relationships that have been formed with supplier/vendors and subcontractors, and these relationships allowed for the agreement of business transactions, resulting in resources, materials and supplies, and equipment and facilities being obtained and used in project activities to accomplish the project objective. As the organization conducts its business and manages projects year after year, it is these relationships that help ensure the organization is successful in its endeavors. These relationships can become stronger as the procurement department gains confidence in the relationship and uses various suppliers/vendors and subcontractors as much as possible based on a good relationship.

In most cases these relationships are built as a result of performance where each party has completed their responsibility in the agreement to the satisfaction of the other party. This relationship, as it improves with each transaction, works to reduce risk for both parties and promotes good business. Procurement departments, upon establishing these relationships, work hard to communicate what is intended in the pricing and delivery negotiations as well as accommodate any special conditions that either side may require to maintain good relationships. The final component that typically ensures a good relationship with a supplier/vendor or subcontractor is final payment, and this is based on the successful delivery of a product or service that meets the expectations of the buyer.

As the project manager and other assisting project staff play important roles in ensuring procurements are being conducted correctly, it's usually at the end of the procurement process when confirmation of delivery is needed before final payment can be made, where stress increases in the relationship between the supplier/vendor, subcontractor, and the organization. The project manager must remember he also has a responsibility in helping to close procurements by actively participating or overseeing the process of verifying procured items have been successfully delivered and meet all the requirements requested. The project manager also needs to communicate this fact to procurement in a timely manner so final payment can be issued. It is important the project manager understand that properly closing procurements is a very important part of the procurement process, and anything he can do to assist in that process will help in not only finalizing that procurement, but in helping to maintain good relationships with suppliers/vendors and subcontractors.

10.2 Evaluate Open Procurements

To effectively evaluate the status of procurements and which procurements need to be closed, it must first be determined which procurements are still open. Depending on the size of the organization and whether the procurement department has processes developed to monitor and control procurements, this can be a simple process or a complex and time-consuming one. We must remember that the procurement department is responsible for purchasing most of what the organization requires for its operation, products, and various projects. This means at any given time there can be hundreds if not thousands of open procurements, and depending on the staffing in the procurements office, it may be difficult to determine what procurements are still open for a given project or work activity.

Some organizations assign a purchasing agent for each project, and that agent is responsible for all procurements throughout the project lifecycle. If this is the case, it is much easier for the project manager and purchasing agent to determine what procurements have been completed and which still remain open. One valuable process tool the project manager can use in conjunction with the procurements department is the *planned procurement monitor* mentioned in Chapter 8, "Procurement Monitoring and Control," which is used to document all planned procurements. This tool can also be used to update the status of progress with each open procurement, as well as view which procurements have been closed and which are still open. Before procurement can be closed, the following steps should be taken not only to verify the status of a particular procurement, but to ensure critical components have been completed.

- **What is still open?**—The first step in closing procurement is to verify the procurement is still open and has not already been classified as complete. This can be a common mistake, as one party assumes that all conditions have been met and feels the procurement is closed, when in reality there are still open actions required and the procurement remains open. If there appears to be actions remaining, it must be clarified if anything has actually been ordered or a contract has actually been signed, and this procurement may be on hold, having not even begun. The purchasing agent must investigate why the procurement is still open and pursue actions to either terminate the procurement if no longer required or to complete open actions to begin progress on the transaction.

- **Verify change order requests**—This is a vital step regarding open procurements where mistakes can be made very easily. As mentioned in earlier chapters, changes can be made during the procurement process that will need to be managed to ensure all of the details required in the change have been communicated to the supplier/vendor or subcontractor, and that they in turn have verified they understand the change order request. It's also important at this point that any required organizational processes for managing change with purchased items, as well as contracts, have been reviewed and are being conducted. As we have seen, change with regard to procurements can be simple or very complex, but all need to be followed up on to ensure corrective actions were completed.

• **Verify all deliveries**—The next step in evaluating open procurements is to determine when items are scheduled to be delivered or when a contractor is scheduled to complete the objective of a contract. At this point in the procurement process, a purchase or contract has already been initiated, and the buyer is either expecting delivery or has already received the product or service. It is important to verify everything that was to be delivered has been received.

10.3 Close Procurements

When the project manager and purchasing agent are reviewing completed procurements, a process needs to be in place that checks off key elements of each procurement to ensure all actions have been completed and the procurement can be officially closed. As the procurement process involves the communication of unintended products or services offered by the seller, the negotiation of pricing and payment terms and conditions, the selection of delivery, and any special conditions that will be required by either party, closing procurements is simply verifying each of these major areas have been completed and satisfies the expectations of each party. Some organizations may have an established process to close procurements, but other organizations simply leave the closing process to the purchasing agent, in which case the project manager should assist in the procurements closing process by performing the following steps:

• **Performance reviews/audits**—As the procurement process can include a wide variety of purchases and services, the general idea in the first step is to review the performance of the supplier/vendor or subcontractor. Although this may not necessarily be an evaluation of pass or fail that affects the final payment, it is valuable information; performance reviews and audits can reveal information about the transaction that might lead to details as to whether the procurement can be closed. In some cases, contracts that are used to manage work from subcontractors may have a performance review component that affects the pay schedule, and in this case the performance review or audit may be required.

In most cases the performance review for a supplier/vendor or subcontractor is for internal use as to whether they would be used in the future. A performance review may shed light on an element of the transaction that may require more investigation as to whether it is in compliance. Performance reviews should always be conducted to categorize or characterize the general conduct and professionalism exhibited by each supplier/vendor and subcontractor.

- **Change requirements review**—Another important element that must be reviewed before procurements can be closed is the evaluation of the outcome of any change requests that were initiated. As we know, change is inevitable, and when change is required in procurements, it is important they are managed and controlled to ensure what is procured is updated to meet the expectations of the buyer. A thorough review of the details of the change is required, as this is a component of verifying the compliance of the final deliverable or service. This can be another area where suppliers/vendors and subcontractors can be graded on performance as to their ability to manage change. Change in procurements also introduces risk and is another important reason why a change requirement review would be necessary before approving the closure of the procurement.

- **Verify compliance of deliverable or service**—The next step needed to close procurements is important to the buyer, which is to confirm that the deliverable or service has met expectations. Where a product has been delivered, inspection should reveal that the product meets all the expectations of quality, form, fit, and function and is undamaged. If the deliverable is a service that is rendered, it must be determined that the service has met the expectations of the buyer and any special conditions have been met. This is one of the most important responsibilities of the buyer, to verify the product or service that was procured has met the expectations of the buyer and therefore final payments can be authorized.

- **Complete payment schedule**—The final step in closing procurements should happen upon verification the product or service has met the expectations of the buyer and any remaining terms or conditions have been satisfied—final payment authorization. This is an important step for the supplier/vendor or subcontractor as this finalizes her side of the transaction. Final payment should never be made unless the buyer is convinced the product or service they have received does meet all of their expectations. In some cases if final payment is held, this allows the buyer leverage to negotiate rework, repairs, or alterations that would bring the deliverable into compliance.

The final payment phase of the transaction is also the most stressful for the seller as this is when the most risk of not getting paid occurs. It's advisable to note for the project manager, purchasing agent, and those in accounting responsible for issuing payments that how the final payment phase is conducted can have an impact on the relationship between the buyer and seller. Once the final payment has been received by the seller and all terms and conditions have been met, the procurement can be officially closed.

- **Early termination**—When we consider the process of closing procurements, in most cases, we are seeing items purchased in contracts carried through their course and completed as expected. One of the major elements of procurements is the risk that things may not always go as planned and how that risk can impact a purchase or a contract. At some point in time the purchasing agent might request to cancel an order or terminate a contract with a subcontractor. This can be for several reasons, some of which may originate from the purchasing department in disagreement with the terms and conditions, or in the case of breach of contract, but in most cases is derived from the request from the project manager and/or project staff. A request for early termination of a purchase or contract can be a result of several factors, including

- Purchase was no longer necessary.
- Item was found through another supplier/vendor at a better price, improved quality, better features, or better delivery schedule.
- Problems due to availability or shipping forced the cancellation of the purchase.
- Contractor did not perform their portion of an agreement to the expectation of the buyer, creating a breach of contract and early termination.
- Scope of work changed such that contractor or buyer was forced to terminate the contract before work started.
- Lack of resources forced in early termination of a contractual agreement.

- **Early purchase termination**—As just noted, there can be several reasons why the purchasing agent or project manager needs to terminate a purchase order before it is filled. This is not to be confused with the return of an item—the item was already received by the buyer and for a reason allowed under the return policy is shipped back to the seller. Early purchase termination refers to cancellation of an order before it is shipped. In the interest of time in a project work activity, this is preferred over waiting for a product to be shipped, only to be returned and then waiting more time for a correct product to be shipped again. If it is determined early that an item selected to be purchased is not correct, early termination of the order allows the correct item to be ordered and shipped with little or no downtime in the work activity.

It must be noted that, depending on what type of items are purchased, when the cancellation is actually initiated, if the seller has not pulled the items from stock and prepared it for shipping, this is easier for the seller, as they have not wasted any time in inventory control and shipping materials. If the item has already been pulled and prepared for shipping, the seller may require a restocking fee to return the item to stock, reimbursing the seller for labor and materials that have been expended.

It is in the best interest of the project manager to make certain all items selected for purchase are correct, as this can avoid an early termination or order cancellation requirement and added time and cost. Unfortunately things change, and this is a risk the project manager may have to consider for each purchased item.

- **Early contract termination**—In the case of contract agreements, these can be more difficult as there are generally statements that detail early termination terms and conditions. These terms and conditions are generally put in a contract to control the risk of one party wanting to simply back out of an agreement, leaving the other party, in most cases, in a perplexing situation. Because this risk can be equally as serious for both buyer and seller, early termination terms and conditions have to be spelled out to protect both parties.

  In the case of the contractor, they are the party that is going out on a limb to expend man-hours, perform work, possibly rent equipment, and purchase materials on good faith that payment will be made in the course of the contract. If the seller (contractor) simply wants to stop activities, the question would be how the seller gets reimbursed for any out-of-pocket expenses already incurred in work activity. This is one of the details that early termination terms and conditions can outline.

  In the case of the buyer, this can be equally as risky, as a subcontractor is scheduled to perform tasks that will represent progress on a work activity, and if that progress is halted prematurely, it can put completion of the work activity at risk. The buyer therefore stipulates terms and conditions of how the contractor can stop work activities and what the contractor needs to do to exit work activities.

  Early termination of contracts are common, but unfortunately contract negotiators are not always skilled in writing terms and conditions to protect the buyer from a contractor wishing to cease activities, leaving the project at risk. Depending on the type of contract, the project manager might want to be aware of what types of early termination terms and conditions each contract might have so she can make note in the risk register how responses may be designed for an early contract termination.

10.4 Claims and Disputes

The final important component in closing procurements is to evaluate any claims or disputes that have been initiated in the procurement process. In some cases, claims or disputes might have been made during a transaction that has to be resolved before final payment can be made. In other cases, the transaction was completed including the final payment, and a claim or dispute was made after the fact. In either case, an issue is now attached to the procurement and needs to be resolved. These types of issues can surface as a result of poor communication, misunderstandings, human error, and even unethical behavior. Regardless of what the root cause of the issue might be, these types of issues fall into one of two general categories: issues regarding the supplier/vendor or an issue relating to a subcontractor.

- **Supplier/vendor**—Claims or disputes involving supplier/vendors can be related to several components of a transaction and can range from being very easy to resolve to extremely complex. The following is a list of areas that are typically the root cause of supplier/vendor issues:
  - Disputes regarding specifications of a product that was purchased
  - Disputes regarding pricing
  - Disputes regarding a change request
  - Claims made for damaged products delivered
  - Disputes regarding poor quality or workmanship of the product
  - Claims made for nonpayment

  These types of issues can keep a procurement transaction open for long periods of time and actually create bigger problems for the organization. It is in the best interest of the project manager, the project, and the procurements department to try to resolve these issues quickly so they will have little or no impact to the project or organization. The best solution to resolving claims and disputes is to seek the advice of one or all of the following: the procurements manager, accounting manager, and upper management skilled in conflict resolution, or possibly obtaining legal counsel if needed.

- **Subcontractor**—The second general category involves claims and disputes involving subcontractors. These types of issues are generally a result of a disagreement in interpreting a particular element within the contract or an issue related to the work being performed. To complicate matters, there is the added component of personality conflict that can create challenges in dealing with the subcontractor. The following is a list of areas that are often at the root of issues regarding subcontractors:
  - Misinterpretation of a term or condition within the contract
  - Misunderstanding in defining a deliverable or work to be performed
  - Late completion of work
  - Disagreement as to the evaluation of quality of work performed
  - Disagreement as to the quality of materials used
  - Misrepresentation of skills and experience by the subcontractor
  - Unethical behavior by either party
  - Disputes over payment amount or payment schedule
  - Legal action taken by one party claiming breach of contract

As with supplier/vendor issues, it is best to seek the advice of skilled and experienced individuals within the organization that can help resolve contractual disputes. These types of problems unfortunately cause procurements to remain open until they can be resolved. In some cases, issues may be negotiated and resolved outside of the project environment where the project manager and project staff would not be involved in the dispute resolution and can progress as scheduled with little or no impact. In many cases with subcontractors, because work being performed is directly involved with the work activity, some contractors can simply stop work until the issue has been resolved, creating problems for the project manager.

With the use of subcontractors, typically project managers include subcontractors as elements of risk in the risk register and design a response should an issue arise with their work. If this is the case, the project manager can simply carry out the risk response to an issue with a subcontractor that can allow progress on the work activity to continue. If there is no plan to replace the contractor from a risk standpoint, it would be in the best interest of the project manager to express concern to those in the organization that can help resolve this issue quickly so work can resume with little impact to the project.

Documentation

The close procurements process is important and needs to be completed throughout each project work activity, but it is also important the project manager and any project staff assisting with procurements document procurements as they are closed. As with everything else on the project, information is gathered throughout the project and is valuable in not only communicating to other project staff, but others in the organization that would benefit from understanding the outcome of various processes conducted on the project. In the case of closing procurements, the procurement department, as well as the accounting department, would benefit from reviewing lessons learned on procurements conducted throughout the project, how change was managed, and the outcome of any disputes or claims made against the organization with regard to procurement.

It is also valuable information for project managers, procurement, and accounting to understand the relationships between suppliers/vendors and subcontractors throughout the project lifecycle. In many cases, the selection of subcontractors is made as a result of past experience in not only the conduct of the subcontractor during the course of the contract period, but also regarding any negotiating experiences that may involve disputes or claims. If contractors were generally pleasant to work with, and even if they had disputes or claims but solved them quickly, they would be considered over other contractors who may have better pricing but are difficult to deal with and who could create more problems than they are worth.

It is also important the project manager and any staff assisting in the project procurement activities, as well as purchasing agents, record information quickly after the occurrence to capture details that may be forgotten if recorded at a later date. Documents that the project manager may update with this valuable information can include

- Procurements management plan
- Risk register
- Preferred supplier/vendor list
- Procurement department records
- Accounting department records
- Lessons learned document

10.5 Summary

As with many other processes performed in project management, procurement has several things that need to be carried out in order to complete the process, and an assessment needs to be made to ensure everything required in the process has been completed. As purchases involve a transaction, two primary components in closing out a purchase are the successful receipt of the item purchased that meets the expectations of the buyer and successful receipt of payment by the seller. As most procurement actions involve purchases, this simple transaction can still be left open due to a variety of reasons.

As we have discussed in this book, there can be several things involved in purchasing an item, and they can all have associated risks. In most cases, human beings are involved in both sides of a purchase transaction and can make mistakes, creating risks. The project manager primarily is interested in making sure the item purchased is delivered on schedule, is undamaged, and meets the expectations of what was required—as well as hitting the price point that was originally estimated. The key component in those items is ensuring the seller has been paid, which is the final closing task of a purchase transaction. As the project manager typically does not issue the payments, this is a forgotten aspect, and transactions can linger open for long periods of time, even creating disputes and legal problems for the organization. The project manager, in having a control function, can make it a point to ensure procurements are closed and payments have been issued to avoid further risk.

If purchases or contract agreements have to be terminated prematurely, the project manager must ensure that an early termination is conducted correctly and is finalized. Canceling orders is common with the procurement department, as changes may need to be made or other circumstances require a purchase to be terminated in the best interest of the project. In the use of contract agreements, early termination may be a result of a breach of contract or a term or condition that was not met by one party or the other. No matter what the cause of an early termination, the project manager is responsible to make sure procurements are closed correctly to finalize the accounting of all monies spent on the project as well as eliminate risk of ongoing issues with open procurements.

10.6 Review Questions

1. Give an example of how a purchased item can still be open after the item has been received by the buyer.

2. Give an example of how a lease agreement for a piece of equipment can remain open after an item has been returned.

3. Discuss an example of how a transaction is properly closed.

4. Give an example of a contract agreement with a subcontractor who was performing work activities that was issued an early contract termination.

5. Discuss how claims and disputes can create problems in closing procurement activities.

10.7 Key Terms

Evaluate open procurements

Close procurements

Early termination

Claims and disputes

Procurement management plan

Risk register

Preferred supplier/vendor list

10.8 PMBOK Connections (5th Ed.)

12.4 Close Procurements

10.9 Case Study Questions (Use Case Study from Chapter 9)

1. Evaluate all open procurements.
2. Perform a vendor audit on the five open contract items.
3. Discuss strategy in closing these procurements.
4. How will contract strategy be used in the best interest of the buyer in closing these procurements?

Bibliography

Barkley, Bruce. *Project Risk Management*. New York, NY: McGraw-Hill, 2004.

Bender, Michael B. *A Manager's Guide to Project Management: Learn How to Apply Best Practices*. Upper Saddle River, NJ: FT Press, 2010.

Cooper, Dale F., Stephen Grey, Geoffrey Raymond, and Phil Walker, *Project Risk Management Guidelines: Managing Risk in Large Projects and Complex Procurements*. West Sussex, England: J. Wiley, 2005.

Evans, James R., William M. Lindsay, and James R. Evans. *Managing for Quality and Performance Excellence*. Mason, OH: Thomson/South-Western, 2008.

Fleming, Quentin W., and Joel M. Koppelman. *Earned Value: Project Management*. 4th ed. Newtown Square, PA: Project Management Institute Inc., 2010.

Garrett, Gregory A. *World Class Contracting*. 5th ed. Chicago, IL: CCH, 2007.

Gido, Jack, and James P. Clements. *Successful Project Management*. 5th ed. Mason, OH: South-Western Cengage Learning, 2012.

Gray, Clifford F., and Erik W. Larson. *Project Management: The Managerial Process*. Boston, MA: McGraw-Hill/Irwin, 2006.

Griffin, Ricky W. *Management*. Boston, MA: Houghton Mifflin, 2005.

Hiegel, James, Roderick James, and Frank Cesario. *Projects, Programs, and Project Teams: Advanced Program Management*. Hoboken, NJ: Wiley Custom Services, 2006.

Kerzner, Harold. *Project Management: A Systems Approach to Planning, Scheduling, and Controlling*. 8th ed. Hoboken, NJ: Wiley, 2003.

Kuehn, Ursula, PMP, EVP. *Integrated Cost and Schedule Control in Project Management*. 2nd ed. Vienna, VA: Management Concepts Inc., 2011.

Morris, Peter W. G., and Jeffrey K. Pinto. *The Wiley Guide to Project Control*. Hoboken, NJ: John Wiley & Sons, Inc., 2007.

Morris, Peter W. G., and Jeffrey K. Pinto. *The Wiley Guide to Project Program & Portfolio Management*. Hoboken, NJ: John Wiley & Sons, Inc., 2007.

Nicholas, John M., and Herman Steyn. *Project Management for Business, Engineering, and Technology: Principles and Practice*. Amsterdam, Netherlands: Elsevier Butterworth Heinemann, 2008.

Pinkerton, William J. *Project Management: Achieving Project Bottom-line Success*. Hightstown, NJ: The McGraw-Hill Companies, Inc., 2003.

Pinto, Jeffrey K. *Project Management: Achieving Competitive Advantage*. 3rd ed. Upper Saddle River, NJ: Pearson Education Inc., 2013.

Project Management Institute. *A Guide to the Project Management Body of Knowledge* (PMBOK® Guide), 5th ed. Newtown Square, PA: Project Management Institute, 2013.

Quantmleap. *"Project Risk Management and the application of Monte Carlo Simulation."* (2010). 12 May 2014. <http://quantmleap.com/blog/2010/07/project-risk-management-and-the-application-of-monte-carlo-simulation/>

Schuyler, John R. *Risk and Decision Analysis in Projects*. Newtown Square, PA: Project Management Institute, 2001.

Vaidyanathan, Ganesh. *Project Management: Process, Technology, and Practice*. Upper Saddle River, NJ: Pearson Education Inc., 2013.

Verma, Vijay K. *Organizing Projects for Success*. Upper Darby, PA: Project Management Institute, 1995.

Wilson, Randal. *A Comprehensive Guide to Project Management Schedule and Cost Control: Methods and Models for Managing the Project Lifecycle*. Upper Saddle River, NJ: Pearson, 2014.

Wilson, Randal. *The Operations Manager's Toolbox: Using the Best Project Management Techniques to Improve Processes and Maximize Efficiency*. Upper Saddle River, NJ: FT Press, 2013.

Index

A

Accept response plan, 133
accepting risk, 131
accounting, 217, 225
activity information checklist, 45-46,
  96-97, 183, 216, 219
activity-level monitoring tools, 188
analysis
  make or buy analysis, 101-106
    internal versus external,
      104-106
    lease or own, 103-104
    make or buy, 101-106
  risk analysis, 31
    basic matrix, 74-75
    decision tree analysis, 78-79,
      84-85
    diagramming methods, 76-77
    overview, 71-73
    qualitative analysis, 74
    qualitative risk assessment
      matrix, 75
    quantitative analysis, 79-85
approving contracts, 222, 224
audits, 225, 252-253
avoiding risk, 131
award phase, 172-173

B

bad risk, 3
baselines, measuring against, 208
basic matrix analysis, 74-75
Beta and Triangular probability
  distributions, 80-83
bibliography, 263
bill of materials (BOM), 97-98
BOM (bill of materials), 97-98

brainstorming, 48
budgetary risk, 54-56
buyers
  contract concerns, 174
  responsibility, 6
  risk, 119-120

C

categorizing risks, 60-65
  change management, 65
  example, 60-61
  Triple Constraint, 61-65
category weighting, 89
cause and effect diagrams, 49-50,
  76-77
CCM (critical chain method), 192-193
change control, 202-208, 225-228
  process, 226
  reasons for change, 202-203
    accepting risk, 203-204
    communicate step, 207
    implement step, 206-207
    measure step, 208
    propose step, 204-206
  subcontractor contracts, 227-228
  supplier/vendor orders, 226-227
change management, 65
  versus problem management, 10-11
  process, 32
change order requests, verifying,
  251-252
change requirements review, 253
checklists
  activity information checklist, 96-97,
    183, 216, 219
  overview, 48-49